MW00580682

Courageous Love:

A Couples Guide to Conquering Betrayal

Dr. Stefanie Carnes

Gentle Path

P R E S S

Gentle Path Press
P.O. Box 2112
Carefree, Arizona 85377
www.gentlepath.com

Copyright © 2020 by Gentle Path Press

All rights reserved. No part of this publication may be used or
reproduced, stored or entered into a retrieval system, transmitted,
photocopied, recorded, or otherwise reproduced in any form by
any mechanical or electronic means, without the prior written
permission of the author, and Gentle Path Press, except for brief
quotations used in articles and reviews.

First edition: 2020

For more information regarding our publications,
contact Gentle Path Press at
1-866-575-6853 (toll-free U.S. only)

ISBN: 978-1-940467-08-5

Library of Congress Control Number: 2020934060

This book is dedicated to the IITAP community. Your passion to help suffering people has been an inspiration for me throughout my career. My gratitude for your support over the years is beyond words. This one is for all of you!

Table of Contents

Acknowledgements

Learning the best approach to treating couples struggling with betrayal has been a long journey with much hard-won knowledge. I would first like to acknowledge the many couples and families that have honored me, by allowing me to be their guide through the healing journey. Their stories and experiences I keep close to my heart and I have tried to share the wisdom gleaned from their experiences throughout this book. Secondly, best practices often emerge as a collective. I have learned so much from other researchers and authors as well as my many colleagues. I would like to acknowledge the many individuals who first started conceptualizing the construct of betrayal trauma. For example, the ground-breaking work of Shirley Glass in her book, *NOT "Just Friends"*, was instrumental in shaping the field. Other researchers and authors that also influenced my perspective included the work of Jennifer Fryed and Judith Herman, in addition to Barbara Steffens and Omar Minwalla, who applied this perspective to the field of sex addiction at a moment that was integral in my personal development. Their timely insight and pioneering work helped pave the way towards a paradigm shift in working with families suffering from betrayal.

I'd also like to thank some of the pioneers in working with partner trauma. First of all, I'd like to acknowledge the ground-breaking work done by Jennifer Schneider and Deb Corley, in addition to Mark and Debbie Laaser. Their research and writing was instrumental in acknowledging the importance of treating the partner in the early days of the field. I'd like to give a special acknowledgement to my friend Kevin Skinner, who I have the privilege to teach alongside on a regular basis. His compassion for partners and couples is unending and his research and writing have made a huge contribution to the field. I'd also like to acknowledge the many therapists who have served as advocates for betrayed partners, many of whom have their own books, workshops, website forums and blogs for partners, including

Sheri Keffer, Dan Drake, Tim Stein, Jeanne Vattuone, Carol Juergensen Sheets, Marnie Breecker, Janice Caudill, Vicki Tidwell Palmer, Michelle Mays, Marnie Ferree, Claudia Black, and Staci Sprout. There are too many partner advocates in our community to mention them all, and I'm grateful for the work you all do for betrayed partners everywhere.

I would also like to acknowledge the many people in our community who have served as betrayed partner advocates, particularly in the realm of teaching, educating and writing about therapeutic disclosure. I'd like to give another special acknowledgement to my friend Mari Lee, whose work in the arena of therapeutic disclosure has been instrumental in moving the field forward. She has also spent tireless hours supporting our community on the listserv, as faculty, and via her work on our ethics committee. Additionally, Dan Drake and Janice Caudill have also done exceptional writing and teaching on the subject of disclosure using a compassionate approach towards betrayed partners. I'd like to thank my friend Barbara Levinson, for her support in creating documents for our IITAP training, in particular, the writing of narrative disclosures, not to mention her tireless and devoted support to IITAP, and her emotional support of me, personally. Additionally, I'd like to mention our dearly departed colleague Brie Bergman, who popularized the "Brie's way" method of disclosure, which was a significant improvement in the structure of the therapeutic disclosure process. Finally I'd like to acknowledge Ken Wells for developing the concept of emotional restitution as part of the healing process.

IITAP would not be what it is without its outstanding faculty: Ken Adams, Alex Katehakis, Debra Kaplan, Kevin Skinner, Greg Futral, Janie Lacey, Erica Sarr, Sheri Keffer, Mari Lee, Adrian Hickmon, Jenna Riemersma, Marnie Ferree, Craig Cashwell and all of our workshop faculty who are too numerous to include. We are so grateful for your passion towards this work and your commitment to teaching excellence. IITAP could not have better instructors!

I'd like to acknowledge those individuals who assisted me in preparation of this manuscript. Thank you to John Gottman, Alex Katehakis, and Kevin Skinner for reading the manuscript prior to its release and for offering their feedback and such wonderful endorsements of this work. I'd also like to acknowledge one of my clients, a betrayed partner who volunteered to proofread the manuscript (you know who you are!). Thank you! And finally, to my editor Scott Brassart. Scott, you are such a gem! I'm so grateful for your work!

Without my team at IITAP, I would not have been able to accomplish this book. Thank you, Jo, Amanda, Tara, Jan, Marina, Arieyana, Jeannine, David and especially Colleen (for her assistance with this manuscript). You guys Rock! Your positive attitudes, commitment to our mission of teaching compassionate and effective treatment to suffering people is a constant source of inspiration. You all plug through the daily grind with enthusiasm for the work, because you know it is meaningful. You work together beautifully and push through our challenges with zest. You guys are the wind at my back and I'm grateful everyday for each of you!

I feel it's important to acknowledge my colleagues from The Meadows. Being invited to be a senior fellow at one of the top facilities in the world in order to create a program for women suffering from intimacy disorders, has been a highlight of my career. I am continually amazed at the incredible depth of the clinical work that we are able to provide as a team. It is such a gift to be part of a team involved in completely transforming lives on a daily basis. I am so honored to be a senior fellow along with so many other amazing leaders in trauma and addiction. To all the administrators, clinicians and the outreach team – thank you for your years of support!

Finally, I'd like to thank my friends and family. Particularly, my loving father, Pat and his wife Pennie, who gave me not only their feedback on this manuscript, but also their love and support. Dad, working with you has been a mountainous adventure with many challenges and peaks and highlights and always an incredible and inspirational view of the world. Thank you for walking this path with me and all of the support along the way! To my children Braiden and Justin, thank you for being patient and understanding when I have to leave town and for being the sunshines of my life. It is so fun to watch you become the incredible men you are becoming. I'm so lucky to be your mom! And finally, to my partner Jose Carlos, thank you for being my rock, my deepest connection, and for always being there when things are hard, and just as importantly, for being there when things are good. You make my life fun and full of excitement and joy.

In writing these acknowledgements, it's apparent to me that I could write pages recognizing all those that have supported my work. How wonderful it is to be part of such an incredible community of people. Thank you all for helping me be courageous!

Stefanie

INTRODUCTION:

An Overview of the Healing Journey

Sexual betrayal is devastating. It shatters the close connection you had with one of the most precious people in your life: your partner. At this moment, while the wound is still fresh, it may be hard to imagine how you and your partner are ever going to put the pieces of the puzzle back together. You may be uncertain about your partner's love for you. You may feel like you're the one to blame. You may feel as though you might never be able to heal, to forgive your partner (or yourself), and move on. You may fear that your relationship will never be the safe, warm, connected haven it once was. You may be afraid that you may not be able to get this connection back and feel unsure about moving forward. You may feel very discouraged and scared.

Whatever it is that you're currently thinking, feeling, and fearing, you should know right now that if you're willing to try to heal yourself and your relationship, you can succeed in that endeavor. If you and your partner are hurting but still truly love each other and want to make it work, that type of healing and restoration is possible. This book can take you on that healing journey.

It is suggested that you and your partner read this book together, study it together, and follow the recommendations together. It is also suggested that you do this with the support of a therapist or, better yet, a therapy team. For example, each of you might have an individual therapist, and together you might have a couples therapist, with all of those therapists communicating as appropriate and working as a team to help you overcome the pain and damage of relationship betrayal.

This book lays out a roadmap that is straightforward and tested for healing after sexual betrayal. It has been used by hundreds of couples successfully. So ask yourself if you still have love in your heart for your partner, and if you are willing to make a solid, focused effort to hold on to the gift of your relationship. If the answer to these questions is yes, then read on.

Here's the thing: True love doesn't come around very often. If you have true love, you have something worth fighting for. But after a sexual betrayal, this fight will require a tremendous amount of internal and external work. You and your partner will be asked to put your egos aside and to come together and communicate on difficult issues.

You will each have to let go of your desire to win the argument. Rather than trying to be right, you will need to put your relationship first, valuing your intimate connection more than your pride. While your process of healing will be difficult, you can hold on to the idea that your partner is the love of your life, and the pain and mistrust you're feeling will pass if you do the necessary work. In the process, you will lay the foundation for a deeper, more intimate feeling of truly knowing and loving one another as a couple.

Before getting deeper into the discussion of relationship betrayal and healing, please be aware that for the remainder of this book the terms 'betrayed partner' will be used to refer to the cheated-on partner and 'participating partner' to refer to the partner who committed the betrayal. If the word 'partner' is used by itself, that means both parties are being spoken to equally.

Throughout this book tasks will be assigned and challenges given to both partners. Completing these tasks and challenges will not be easy. At times, a significant amount of work will be involved. Many of the assignments will ask you to put your pride and heartbreak aside and to prioritize your relationship over yourself. You also be asked to step into your relationship emotionally, rather than withdrawing, as you will probably want to do at least occasionally.

This work will require a leap of faith on your part, as you may be pretty unsure about your relationship at the moment. One minute you love your partner deeply and can't imagine life apart; the next minute you can't stand to even be in the same house. Either way, you will be consistently asked to give it your all as you two try to save the love that you have.

Before proceeding, you need to understand that there may have been dysfunction in your relationship prior to the betrayal. All couples have cycles of dysfunction in which both parties play a part. If you are the participating partner, this book will ask you to push that aside for the moment—knowing full well that this may be one of the most difficult things you do during the healing process. You will be asked to do this because, at this time, healing from the betrayal you committed is the most important issue in your relationship. As part of that healing process, your betrayed partner needs you to take the first step by accepting full responsibility for your actions.

Later in the book, in Chapter 9, the process of healing other issues in your relationship will be discussed. At that point in time you can drill down and examine the causes of your behavior, such as shame, trauma, family issues and addiction. For now, however, and throughout the bulk of this book, the focus will be on healing the immediate betrayal, as the pain of that betrayal supersedes all other issues.

Note to Participating Partners

You cannot ask your betrayed partner to take partial blame for your actions. You need to take full and complete responsibility for the betrayal. You must strive to heal the damage wrought by your betrayal before you try to address other issues. You must take the first steps toward healing by owning the pain you've caused your betrayed partner and your relationship. Later, when the betrayal has been adequately addressed, you can look at other issues that impact you and your partner.

While you are working on this process of healing, both of you are encouraged to not make threats that you're leaving the relationship. When you feel hurt, rejected, or like your needs aren't getting met in your relationship, you may, in the heat of the moment, want to make threats to leave. However, these barbs, thrown out in a fit of anger, cause further distrust and erosion of your already damaged bond. So make the decision to commit to the work and don't allow those threats to leave your lips. This restraint will require self-containment and control if things get heated and emotional—and they will—so please make a deeply concerted effort. If you feel like you are getting emotionally flooded, ask your partner for a time out and step away until you're able to calm down a bit.

How To Use This Book

As stated above, it is strongly recommended that both partners engage in individual therapy or counseling during this difficult time, to help manage some of the intense emotions you may be feeling. Couples counseling is also recommended to help with communication, boundaries, and other issues.

- Participating partners should get support from an individual therapist and an accountability team.
- Betrayed partners should get support from an individual therapist and a support team.
- Your relationship should get support from a couples therapist who can help with day-to-day relationship issues and longer-term changes.

Throughout this book, different examples of sexual betrayal will be used. This could be in the form of an affair, casual sex, hookups, webcamming, online or real-world flirting, pornography, sex and porn addiction, or anything else that violates the sexual and romantic boundaries of your relationship. The healing strategies contained in the book are relevant for all of these situations, so please read with that in mind. Rather than searching for the differences between your situation and the examples utilized, look for the similarities.

There are some couples who are not appropriate for this process:

- If one or both parties has an active addiction
- If either party is seriously mentally unstable
- If either party is participating in violent or abusive behavior
- If either party has filed for divorce and there are financial and legal complications

In other words, this book is for couples who are committed to recovery and to making their relationship work.

An Overview of the Healing Process

The process of healing from betrayal is actually straightforward. The path is clear, but also rocky and difficult to navigate. First and foremost, both partners need to understand the traumatic nature of betrayal. For betrayed partners, learning about infidelity is often the most painful and hurtful experience of their entire life. The one person in their life they thought they could trust no matter what has betrayed them.

Let's be clear: The vast majority of betrayed partners are traumatized. It's like they just found out they've got cancer. The mere thought of it is overwhelming. So they swing from one emotional extreme to another. One moment they're calm and invested in the solution; the next moment, they're so angry that they can't even speak.

Meanwhile, participating partners may actually be feeling relief about the fact that their cheating (or some of it, anyway) is finally out in the open. Now they can start being truthful and stop living a double life. They can work toward healing themselves and their relationship, and they can release the heavy load of shame they're carrying about the infidelity.

Because participating partners are suddenly starting to feel better, they may struggle to understand their betrayed partner's up and down, highly emotional reactions. They may think that saying "I'm sorry" is enough and their betrayed partner should just accept that apology and move forward with the process of healing. When that doesn't happen—and it won't—the participating partner may get defensive and push blame onto the betrayed partner for his or her choice to cheat.

So, one of the first steps toward healing is for both partners to understand that the betrayed partner is *traumatized*, and traumatized individuals just don't forgive and let go. Traumatized people are *in crisis* and respond accordingly. They pull it together for a little while, and then they fall apart. They point fingers and get angry, then they internalize blame and fall into a funk, then they get super busy and productive, then they… well, you get the point. And if both partners do not fully understand that this is a *normal and expected reaction* by the betrayed partner, the process of healing the relationship is considerably more difficult.

Honesty is the next key element of recovery. Participating partners rarely want to become fully honest about their behavior. Sometimes this is because they don't want to make their betrayed partner angrier and more reactive than he or she already is. Other times, they don't want to cause their betrayed partner to feel more emotional anguish. Usually, it's a combination of both of these (and maybe a few other) reasons.

Betrayed partners, in most cases, want to know everything, and they want to know it right now. They won't be able to begin the process of starting to trust their participating partner again until they get what they want—the truth. This book walks both partners through the process of getting honest (officially known as therapeutic disclosure).

Once you're past these incredibly important initial stages of healing and recovery, you can move into specific aspects of healing and rebuilding intimacy. This process involves the following, often incredibly difficult, tasks:

- Sharing and listening
- Experiencing empathy
- Grieving
- Making emotional restitution
- Healing the sexual relationship
- Addressing other relationship issues
- Moving forward

So, as stated earlier, the road of relationship repair is logical and straightforward, but it is not easy. Both partners are likely to experience extremes of emotion and thinking along the way. Both partners, at times, are likely to wonder, *Is this worth the pain and effort?* And that is okay. It's normal. It's a part of the journey that you can and will overcome as long as you both keep in the forefront of your mind your desire to stay together, to rebuild trust, and to experience new feelings of love, connection, and intimacy.

CHAPTER ONE:

Understanding the Traumatic Nature of Betrayal

Common Reactions to Betrayal

It is imperative for both partners to understand that when the participating partner engages romantically or sexually outside of the relationship, it is incredibly traumatic for the betrayed partner. Romantic and sexual infidelity are betrayals of the most fundamental nature, and these behaviors uproot the core of the attachment and connection you have with one another.

It is critical that the participating partner understands how painful and destabilizing this is for the betrayed partner. It's just as critical for the betrayed partner to understand that the devastation he or she is feeling is a normal response. In fact, many betrayed partners, after learning about the betrayal, exhibit symptoms of post-traumatic stress disorder (PTSD) and acute stress disorder.[1, 2]

Information about the more common betrayal trauma reactions with betrayed partners is provided below.

Intense Shame

Many betrayed partners feel a sense of unworthiness after betrayal. They feel that something is wrong with them, that the infidelity occurred because they aren't good enough in some way. When other people learn about the betrayal (friends and family), betrayed partners may feel like those people agree with that assessment, that they are judging the betrayed partner and assuming the participating partner cheated because the betrayed partner wasn't attractive enough, sexual enough, attentive enough, etc. Betrayed partners also worry that others will judge them for choosing to stay in the relationship.

Shame, the internalized belief that one is inherently defective and not good enough, plays into and is exacerbated by these fears. Shame is an extraordinarily uncomfortable emotion that both causes and increases intense suffering. It's not uncommon for betrayed partners to try to medicate their pain through substance use or abuse, binge eating, and other self-soothing and potentially addictive behaviors.

Betrayed partners, it's important that you recognize that your partner's infidelity is not about your worth or value as a person. Work with your therapist to recognize that any shame you may be carrying about this is not yours to carry. You are worthy of love and it's important that you don't internalize a sense of worthlessness as a result of your partner's destructive behaviors.

Self-Blame

In addition to feeling shame, betrayed partners may blame themselves for the infidelity. They may think that if they had been a better partner or more sexually available, the cheating wouldn't have happened.

Self-blame is actually a common behavior in trauma victims of all types. You might hear rape victims say that if they hadn't been drunk at that party or wearing that short skirt, the rape wouldn't have happened. Or people diagnosed with a serious physical illness wonder if their eating habits, a lack of exercise, and a stressful lifestyle caused the illness. Sometimes this type of thinking causes people to think they 'deserve' the trauma that has occurred; they think they somehow earned it.

It is normal to wonder what you could have done to prevent something awful from happening. This is especially likely for betrayed partners because all couples have areas of dysfunction. The betrayed partner can easily feel that whatever was not working in the relationship is the cause of the betrayal and that it is entirely his or her fault. That is not, however, the case. Lingering problems in a relationship belong to both parties. More importantly, it was the participating partner's choice to be unfaithful.

This does not mean that the relationship dysfunction that existed before the betrayal doesn't eventually need to be addressed. In fact, it is imperative to address this dysfunction (there is more about this in Chapter 9). It is recommended, however, that this work be put off until after you've worked through the bulk of the healing process surrounding betrayal that is outlined in this book.

Confusion

Most betrayed partners are confused about what really happened. As such, they want the complete truth about everything that took place. This is a normal response to the secrets, lies, and gaslighting perpetrated by the participating partner.

Gaslighting, in case you're unfamiliar with the term, is a form of psychological abuse that involves the presentation of false information followed by dogged insistence that the information is true. Over time, gaslighting causes betrayed partners to feel crazy and to question their perception of reality. With gaslighting, betrayed partners feel like they can't trust their gut instincts. Gaslighting victims have thoughts like, *There's all sorts of evidence that says you're cheating, but you keep insisting that you're not, so maybe you're not. Maybe I'm making things up in my head.*

Participating partners keep secrets, tell elaborate lies, and engage in gaslighting behaviors for several reasons:

1. They want to continue their behavior, so they need to cover up their actions.
2. They don't want to hurt their partner, so they try to cover their tracks and hide the behavior.

3. For some participating partners, psychological factors such as trauma, addiction, entitlement, sociopathy, and family of origin issues could be contributing to their behavior.

Unfortunately, secrets, lies and gaslighting have the completely opposite effect. Betrayed partners often know something is amiss long before they *know* something is amiss. And when they do find out about the betrayal, they are devastated by the deception.

When secrets, lies, and gaslighting are part of the betrayal—and they nearly always are—it is normal for betrayed partners to be confused about reality. In these circumstances, they are highly likely to ask for (or demand) the truth about all of the infidelity and deceptive behavior. They ask for this so they can reclaim their reality.

For betrayed partners, knowing what happened is like putting the individual pieces of a puzzle together to see the real picture. So betrayed partners will repeatedly question participating partners about their behavior, asking for details and going over the story again and again to make sure they understand. They want the complete truth so they can understand the scope of the betrayal and move forward based on that knowledge.

The therapeutic process of full disclosure is discussed in Chapter 3. For now, to put it simply, attempting full disclosure without therapeutic assistance is not recommended.

Fear and Hypervigilance

After experiencing secrets, lies, and other forms of deception, it is normal for betrayed partners to fear they're losing the relationship, and to feel anxiety about the fact that the participating partner may still be cheating. As a result, many betrayed partners will want to keep tabs on the participating partner's whereabouts and behavior. They may participate in detective-type behaviors. They may check electronic devices for communication with acting out partners, track financial activity, use an app that tracks the participating partner's location, etc.

These actions are 'safety seeking' behaviors. The betrayed partner wants to feel safe, and it seems like the only way to do that is to make sure the infidelity is not continuing and the participating partner is not still lying and keeping secrets. The majority of betrayed partners manifest this type of hypervigilant response, and it is important for both partners to know that this is a normal and relatively expected reaction to betrayal trauma.

Lack of Social Support

Usually, when someone experiences a major trauma, such as a major medical event or a car accident, friends and family rally around this person and support them. But in the case of sexual betrayal, many couples feel like they can't tell anyone, lest they be judged. However, getting support through this trial—as with any other major trauma—is essential. In fact, both research and clinical experience tell us that a key element in overcoming trauma of any type is not going through it alone.

When traumatized people get acknowledgment and support from family, friends, therapists, etc., the trauma loses its power and they're able to heal. When they don't, the trauma festers inside them, oftentimes turning into shame—the inherent belief that they are defective, unworthy, less than, and unlovable. So reaching out to empathetic and supportive others after the trauma of intimate betrayal is vital to the process of healing.

For betrayed partners, participating in a therapy group for betrayal trauma is an excellent option because the other group members will have experienced similar trials and difficulties. For participating partners, getting into a 12-step recovery group or program is appropriate if the behavior was addictive in nature. If not, participating partners can look for a therapy group or accountability group for people who have been unfaithful and want to repair their relationship.

Both partners should find a few trusted people—nonjudgmental friends, family, and a therapist—to share their struggles and provide guidance. Sharing about the infidelity with everyone in your entire support system, is not recommended, however, at least not until some time has passed and the process of healing is well underway.

Sometimes couples will overshare and later regret that everyone knows their secrets. The shame and the stigma of struggling with betrayal can be immense, and, at times, both of you will want to not think about it and to go about your daily lives as normal. If everyone you know is aware of the infidelity, however, that's not so easy.

That said, it is important to have at least a few trustworthy people with whom you can openly talk about the betrayal. Choose people who will not judge you or offer unsolicited advice. It is recommended that you choose people who, in a general way, are supportive of your relationship. These are the individuals most likely to help you make smart decisions about what is right for you. If your mom never liked your significant other, for example, she's probably not a good person to turn to because she will likely judge you for staying and strongly push you to break things off. Your best friend, on the other hand, who just wants you to be happy, could be a solid choice.

Public Embarrassment

Unfortunately, there are times when your community is aware of the pain and anguish you are experiencing in your relationship. When information about the betrayal is public in this way, it creates a second source of pain for both partners. The betrayed partner is likely to feel judged by others—as not being a good enough spouse, or as doing something to drive the participating partner to adultery, etc. This can lead to feelings of intense shame and embarrassment. The participating partner might feel similar judgment and shame.

In such cases, it is helpful, if possible, to come together and support each other through this public trial. In most cases, it is best for the participating partner to simply take full accountability and responsibility in these circumstances. At the very least, that can relieve some of the unwarranted judgment and shame felt by the betrayed partner. It is also wise to set boundaries to help you deal with people who inquire about your relationship on a too personal level. Most couples choose to simply say that this is something they are trying to work through, and they'd appreciate others respecting their privacy while they recover and heal.

Grief

When there is sexual betrayal, there are serious consequences and losses. In addition to losses in your primary relationship, there may be losses with other relationships, such as lost friendships if the betrayal occurred with people you knew. There could also be health consequences, such as STDs or illness caused by the stress of betrayal. There could be financial losses related to the betrayal itself (hotel rooms, drugs, money for prostitution, etc.), plus the costs of therapy and legal fees in the aftermath. Worst of all, there could be pain caused to your children—regardless of whether they know about the betrayal—because children innately sense, and often internalize, turmoil within the family.

Ultimately, you may wonder if the safe, connected relationship that you once had has been nothing more than a farce. You may feel that the dreams you had for a long and enjoyable life with your partner are out of reach. You may worry that you will never again feel safety, love, and intimate emotional connection with your partner. You may fear that all or part of your relationship is over. At the very least, you may need to grieve the loss of your old relationship as you work on building a new relationship with your partner.

Forging a new and better relationship is not an impossible task. Many couples who have healed from the devastation of betrayal have come back stronger than ever. Often, the couples that survive betrayal are changed in deeply and profoundly positive ways. They find a new level of intimacy and respect for one another. A great relationship is still possible; your success is up to you.

Emotional Instability

Betrayed partners often find that, after learning about the betrayal, they have difficulty functioning in their daily life. They may feel anxious or depressed. They may experience difficulty working or concentrating. Symptoms like crying spells, feeling a lack of motivation, difficulty sleeping, and having health problems are all common reactions to learning about intimate betrayal.

If you're experiencing this, it is very important that you pay attention to your state of wellness. Eating well, getting enough (but not too much) sleep, and practicing meticulous self-care can help carry you through. Practicing meditation, exercising, and doing activities such as yoga and tai chi can be extremely helpful. At the same time, you should stay away from self-defeating behaviors such as substance abuse, binge eating, and overspending. Participating in therapy and a support group is also very important.

If you find that you cannot function in your daily life, visiting a psychiatrist for medication to help you through this difficult time is recommended. You can always work with your doctor to come off your medication when your stress level goes down.

Anger

Naturally, most betrayed partners are extremely angry post-discovery. And why not? The person they thought they could trust the most has let them down in the most painful of ways. As a betrayed partner, it is absolutely normal to be furious that your participating partner has disrespected you and jeopardized your relationship (and everything else in your life that's important) in such a profound way.

For many betrayed partners, the agony of infidelity turns into bitterness and criticism, which are variations of anger. Sometimes angry betrayed partners are so hurt that their anger manifests as verbal or even physical abuse. When one is wounded so deeply, it is normal to want to lash out in reaction. That said, retaliation—verbal or otherwise—is counterproductive to the process of healing your relationship.

Recognizing this fact, it is important that both of you agree to something that you will likely, at various points in your process of healing, find incredibly difficult. *Please do not be verbally abusive, retaliatory, or shaming towards one another.* When you are furious, perhaps with good reason, this request is going to be a tall order. However, it is in the best interest of your relationship if you can express your anger in a healthy and productive way rather than dysfunctionally.

There is a difference between being rightfully angry and assertive versus being abusive, rageful, and vengeful. If your response to rightful anger crosses the line and becomes abusive, that can be horribly damaging to the sense of intimate emotional attachment in your relationship—the very thing you are trying to heal and restore.

Many couples dealing with betrayal struggle with anger, despite their best efforts. This is actually quite normal, and you will likely experience this to some degree in your own process of healing. It is helpful to work on this in individual counseling, as well as in couples counseling. With attention and effort, you can learn to share your anger in an effective, functional, and empowering manner instead of a destructive one.

This level of restraint may require a tremendous amount of work and effort, but if you can manage it, both you and your relationship will reap the benefits. Ultimately, if you can take the high road and respond to feelings of anger effectively, you will feel better about yourself, as your responses will honor who you truly are as a person (and not who you are when you're reacting out of anger). You will also feel better about your relationship as you learn to resolve your conflicts productively.

Avoidance and Distraction

After learning about betrayal, many couples just want life to return to normal. Often, they will throw themselves back into the usual routine, focusing on business and parenting and just returning to the basic grind. It's actually normal to not want to think about your problems and to move on with your life. The ability to do this is a strength and resiliency skill that can help you get through most traumatic events. But like many strengths, it can also be an Achilles heel, especially when dealing with relational traumas.

With betrayal trauma, it is unwise to go into hyper-drive with life to avoid facing the stress and other forms of emotional discomfort you are feeling. Betrayed partners who go into super-functional mode, without practicing self-care and getting support, tend to become physically ill. The stress of making it through the day while pretending nothing is wrong is just too much to handle. Your body and mind need conscientious care and support, not distraction, when you're walking through the stress of betrayal trauma.

Ambivalence and Withdrawal

Whether you are the betrayed partner or the participating partner, you may, in the moment, be uncertain about your relationship. You don't want to be hurt and you don't want to cause hurt, and you don't know how to proceed without pain. As such, it's not uncommon for one or both partners to emotionally withdraw, fearing that things will not work out.

Betrayed partners may not be sure they'll be able to trust the participating partner ever again. If so, they may wonder if they should stay to try to work things out or break it off. Participating partners may wonder the same thing from the other side of the equation: *Will I ever be trusted again, and, if not, what should I do?*

The good news is that at this early stage of the process you don't need to make a final decision about whether you want to stay or go. In fact, it is suggested that you don't even attempt to make that decision right now. Trying to do everything you can to restore your relationship is a worthwhile and long process. It's best to stay away from decision-making and give your all to the process of healing.

As you do this, please keep in mind the commitments you have been asked to make—to not make threats to leave the relationship, and to express your anger productively rather than dysfunctionally.

Case Example: Mario and Rosa

Mario and Rosa entered therapy after Rosa learned that Mario was having an affair with a woman in their apartment complex. She had suspected he might be cheating at numerous points in their 22-year marriage, but he always denied it. He told her she was being paranoid, and he would never even think about cheating on her. But then she found nude pics of the neighbor woman on Mario's phone.

Rosa says that at first she was too much in shock to be angry. She simply confronted Mario with the images and the accompanying texts and sexts she'd found. As usual, Mario denied any wrongdoing, saying the neighbor woman was pursuing him and he'd been telling her no and asking her to stop. But that assertion was undermined by the lengthy history of texts and sexts both received and sent.

For Rosa, it was Mario's lies, even when he was confronted with direct evidence of his cheating, that sent her over the edge. Years of fear and confusion bubbled to the surface and erupted as rage, and she insisted that Mario pack a bag and leave the house immediately, which he eventually agreed to do. He has been staying with his brother since that time.

Mario now swears he's ended the affair. He also insists it's the only time he's ever cheated, and that it didn't mean anything to him emotionally.

Rosa says her emotions are all over the place. One minute she's furious and never wants to see Mario again; the next minute she misses him desperately and wants him back. She says she is willing to work on repairing the relationship, but only if Mario is willing to come clean and tell her everything. She also says she knows there is more to tell because she checked the search history on the family computer and found evidence of sexual encounters, including encounters with prostitutes set up through the internet and various hookup sites. She also says that on Mario's credit card history there are hotel rooms, dinners, and other expenses that she did not know about.

Mario has spoken with his brother about the situation, but Rosa has not shared her anger, fear, and grief with anyone. She says she is afraid that her friends and family will think the cheating is her fault because she's not a good enough wife, or she doesn't give Mario enough sex or the types of sex that a man needs to be happy, or that she's simply not attractive anymore. Worse yet, she says that a lot of the time she believes these negative thoughts, thinking that if she was prettier or more fun, then Mario would never have cheated.

Rosa says she's struggling with her feelings and can't control them. She also can't seem to make decisions—about anything. She struggles to get to sleep, and when she does fall asleep, she has a hard time waking up. She says she doesn't feel safe at home or in the world. She doesn't trust Mario or anyone else she encounters. She's short-tempered at work, with the kids, and with Mario. She also says that her only coping mechanism is to medicate her feelings with food, and she's gained 10 pounds in less than a month.

Rosa's up and down reactions to learning about Mario's betrayal are perfectly normal. Before any true relationship healing can take place, both Mario and Rosa need to accept that Mario's infidelity has *traumatized* Rosa, and she's not going to get over it overnight. No matter how crazy and unpredictable Rosa's emotions seem to Mario, he will need to stop blaming her for having them. At the same time, Rosa will need to stop beating herself up for being emotional and feeling unstable.

Once both partners *accept* the traumatic nature of the betrayal, they can *address* the trauma and move forward into healing. This begins with the betrayed partner identifying and communicating immediate safety needs.

Identifying Immediate Needs

Betrayed partners such as Rosa have immediate needs when they first learn about betrayal.

- They need to feel a sense of safety in the relationship.
- They need to feel that the participating partner is willing to change, willing to make a serious commitment to behaving differently.
- They need to feel that the cheating has stopped.
- They need to feel that repair of the relationship is the participating partner's number one priority.

To this end, betrayed partners typically want to see some immediate and basic changes before they consider moving forward with the process of healing and restoring the relationship. These initial changes are non-negotiable boundaries.

Examples of initial non-negotiable boundaries include:

- I need you to sever ties with your affair partner by letting that person know I am aware of the affair, and you are committed to saving your relationship with me.
- I need you to ask your affair partner never to contact you again.
- I need to install filtering/monitoring/tracking software on all of your digital devices, including phones and other mobile devices.
- I need you to commit to intensive couples therapy so we can work toward repairing the damage done to our relationship.
- I need you to sleep in the guest room while I work through some of my pain and anger about the betrayal.
- I need for us to start working toward therapeutic disclosure of everything that was involved in the betrayal.
- I need for you to engage in treatment for your sex or pornography addiction.

Communicating Immediate Needs

Once a betrayed partner has identified his or her immediate needs and initial non-negotiable boundaries, these need to be shared with the participating partner.

The betrayed partner should ask the participating partner to agree to a time to discuss these needs and boundaries. If the two of you are already in couples therapy, you can have this conversation in your next session. If not, you should schedule a time to meet and talk within the next few days. It is important to understand that these needs of the betrayed partner are *immediate*, so you should not put this conversation off. This discussion needs to happen sooner rather than later, even if you are both deeply mired in pain and anger.

In this meeting, it is suggested that the two of you work together to create two lists that you will use as guidance in the early stages of healing. Before you start working on your lists, however, please keep in mind and consider the following statement.

> The two of you have the power to heal your pain and restore this relationship. Take this time together to put the needs of your relationship first, giving them priority over your individual issues and desires. Rather than fighting each other, fight the infidelity and work together to save your relationship.
>
> Making a commitment to restoring your relationship is going to take work and sacrifice. It may mean taking actions and making commitments that are difficult.
>
> Please attempt to commit to one another to have true compassion and empathy for one another. Try to put yourselves in each other's shoes. Please also commit to treating one another with respect, and to speaking with compassion and kindness.
>
> This doesn't mean you have to agree about everything. It means you can honor one another with respectful communication and compassion and work toward reaching a compromise on important issues.
>
> This is a way for you to honor yourselves and your love for each other as you work toward healing your relationship.

After reading this statement, you can begin work on your two lists.

The first list involves non-negotiable boundaries that will help the betrayed partner feel safe while affirming the participating partner's commitment to the relationship. Non-negotiable boundaries usually involve requests to demonstrate that the acting out has ceased, and requests to help the partner feel secure in the relationship. Betrayed partners, you should work to create this list alone, or with the support of your therapist. Once you have identified your non-negotiable boundaries, you can share them with your partner. The participating partner will need to honor the boundaries that are agreed upon. You may want to share your list in the presence of your couples therapist for support.

Ultimately, this list describes the betrayed partner's needs, but the participating partner should feel free to make suggestions that he or she feels might support the betrayed partner and provide reassurance. It is unwise for the participating partner to argue against any boundaries that the betrayed partner would like to implement. Early on, betrayed partners need reassurance and support that the acting out has ended. The participating partner's willingness to do whatever it takes to demonstrate their commitment to the healing of the relationship is paramount.

Please list the boundaries you agree upon in the space below. Keep in mind that all of your agreed-upon boundaries should support the highest good for the relationship while providing reassurance to the betrayed partner. Betrayed partners, ask yourselves, "What do I need to feel safe in this relationship?" Participating partners, ask yourselves, "What can I commit to that will provide my partner with safety and reassurance?

In the space below, list your non-negotiable boundaries.

....

....

....

....

....

....

....

When your relationship is weakened by sexual betrayal, it is helpful to have positive experiences that counterbalance some of the negative feelings that the two of you experience. Research has shown that having a ratio of more positive experiences than negative experiences is important in a relationship.[3] When you are struggling as a couple, it may be hard to think about going out and having fun together, but please consider things that you could do that would increase your positive interactions as a couple. Could you set aside differences and try to put the betrayal on a shelf and continue to spend time together in a productive way?

Here are some examples:

- We agree to spend quiet time in nature, hiking, gardening, or going to the beach.
- We agree to go see a movie together once a week.
- We agree to have tea together in the evenings and try to connect about the day.
- We agree to watch our favorite funny YouTube videos together a few times per week.

There may be times when one of you may be upset and may not feel like participating in these activities, and that's understandable. Or there may be times when the stress is high in the relationship, and you may have to take a break with these behaviors. In general, though, trying to keep some positivity in your relationship will be helpful for your coupleship. To this end, your next list is actions you are willing to take as a couple as part of your commitment to saving your relationship. To get started, evaluate the quality time you spend together. Ask yourselves: What do we enjoy doing together? What experiences have brought us closer in the past? What passions or hobbies do we share?

In the space below, list the actions you are willing to take as a couple as part of your commitment to your relationship.

....

....

....

Courageous Love

....

....

....

....

....

....

CHAPTER TWO:

Getting Honest

The Need for Truth

A clever definition of intimacy is *into me you see*. Intimacy promotes closeness, connection, openness, vulnerability, and belonging. These are traits that we all naturally crave and desire, and they are essential in a primary love relationship. Secrets, lies, gaslighting, and other forms of emotional and psychological manipulation are the opposite of intimacy. Intimacy is driven by truth and feelings freely shared. Secrecy drives disconnection, guilt, shame, loneliness, and emotional isolation.

Participating partners become masters of secrecy. Oftentimes, they keep secrets because they are afraid their sexual betrayal will create pain and anger in their betrayed partner. They fear the truth because the truth might result in the loss of their relationship. What they don't realize is that their secrets, lies, and deception are usually more painful and anger-inducing than the behavior they're covering up. They fail to understand that betrayed partners generally are more upset about the ongoing deceit than any particular sexual activity that took place.

Meanwhile, betrayed partners *need* the truth to make sense of what happened and reclaim their reality. They need to know exactly what happened and how they were deceived to create a baseline of reality from which they can move forward. Without this starting point for healing, they often feel stuck.

The betrayed partner's biggest fears, after learning about infidelity, center on what they don't know. Should they be worried about STDs? Are there financial issues they don't know about? Did the cheating involve someone they know and trust, like a friend, sibling, or neighbor? To be honest, the list of unanswered questions is almost endless, and until the betrayed partner knows the complete truth about the betrayal, the questions will keep coming. If those questions are not answered, the betrayed partner can't help but make up worst-case scenarios that typically are far worse than the actual truth.

At this point, you might be thinking, *Isn't it traumatic for partners to receive full disclosure of information about the betrayal?* The answer to that is yes, it is, but in most cases it is necessary. If you hope to heal your damaged relationship and rebuild intimacy, the betrayed partner needs a foundation of honesty from which he or she can move forward, and both partners need for relationship trust to be restored. Both of these prerequisites to healing require full disclosure about the betrayal.

There are some partners (usually a small minority), that do not want any information about the acting out. In those cases, the betrayed partner's wishes should always be honored. If they change their minds, their questions can always be answered at a later point in time.

Dysfunctional Disclosures

Unfortunately, not all forms of disclosure are helpful. In fact, some forms of disclosure do more harm than good. One of the most dysfunctional disclosure patterns is referred to as staggered disclosure.

Staggered disclosure typically starts when the betrayed partner finds out about some aspect of the cheating. The participating partner attempts to minimize the impact of his or her betrayal by only admitting to the minimum amount of information—what the betrayed partner already knows about. When asked if there is more, the participating partner lies and says that what the betrayed partner already knows is the full extent of the betrayal. Then the betrayed partner discovers more information and the process repeats. The betrayal is revealed slowly, over many weeks or months, in small amounts, which is devastating to the betrayed partner and the relationship.

Another highly dysfunctional form of disclosure occurs when the participating partner dumps all of the information at once to assuage his or her guilt. Other times this occurs because the betrayed partner says he or she wants to know everything *immediately* and won't take no for an answer. Either way, neither partner is prepared for the pain of this information dump. Neither partner has the emotional strength and external support that is needed to healthfully process and work through the pain of this type of disclosure.

Generally speaking, characteristics of dysfunctional disclosures include:

- The disclosure is not done with therapeutic guidance.
- Information is shared when neither party has a support network in place.
- The disclosure is not followed up with a supportive healing process to help mend the rupture in the relationship.
- Disclosure is piecemeal, with information coming out over time.
- Information is shared only when the betrayed partner discovers it on his or her own.
- Information is dumped all at once to assuage the participating partner's guilt.
- Unnecessary details are shared, increasing the betrayed partner's PTSD symptoms.
- Overly graphic language is used to describe what happened, increasing the betrayed partner's PTSD symptoms.
- Information is not shared in an organized fashion, and therefore is confusing for the betrayed partner.
- Information is shared using slang or jargon that is either too graphic or confusing for the betrayed partner.
- Information is shared when the betrayed partner is too vulnerable or fragile to hear and process it (for example, during a period of severe illness or psychiatric instability).
- Information is shared after the couple has decided to split up.
- The disclosure is not complete, leaving out important details that will upset the partner when they emerge later.

Case Example: Eddie and Maxine

Eddie and Maxine are childhood sweethearts who got married right out of high school. They had four kids in their first six years of marriage. Eddie had a good job, and Max stayed home to be with the kids. When their youngest child reached school age, Max suddenly found herself home alone with little to do beyond cleaning the house and preparing meals. Because Eddie was making good money, she did not need to work, and they both agreed that her efforts were best focused on the family, especially the kids and their needs.

To fill her free time, Max got very involved in social media – primarily Facebook and Instagram. At first, she connected with old friends and family who'd moved away, and she posted lots of pics of her and Eddie and the kids. She felt like this was a form of scrapbooking, a way of documenting her life and the life of her family. Before long, however, Jeremy, a man she'd dated before Eddie, contacted her to say hello and to see how she was doing. After a few months of chatting, Jeremy told Max that he was going to be back in their hometown for a business trip, and he asked if she wanted to have lunch while he was there. Max saw no reason not to do that, so they met.

At their lunch, Max shared with her ex about how bored she was just being a wife and mother. He said he had similar feelings about his own life and marriage. Nothing sexual happened at that meeting, but an emotional boundary was crossed, and from that point on, Max was more likely to turn to Jeremy with her important thoughts and feelings than Eddie. And Jeremy was more likely to turn to Max than his wife. Within a year, their emotional affair became sexual, with Max traveling to the city where Jeremy lived (an hour away), ostensibly to shop, but really to spend time with Jeremy, and Jeremy traveling to their hometown, ostensibly to see friends and family, but really to spend time with Max.

Eventually, Max put her profile on a few hookup apps as well as on social media, and her infidelity took off in earnest, with countless dates and hookups while Eddie was at work and the kids were in school.

Eddie found out about one of Max's hookups about six months ago when he saw her having what appeared to be a romantic lunch with a strange man. That night he confronted her and asked what was going on. At first, Max said the man was an old family friend, and she was just catching up with him, but when Eddie asked to see Max's phone, she refused. She did, however, admit that her lunch was a 'get to know you' date, and she only lied about it because she didn't want to hurt Eddie's feelings. She also said she only did it because she was bored with her life, that she'd never done anything like that before, and it would never happen again.

At that point, Eddie began to engage in safety seeking behaviors in an attempt to find out the truth. He monitored Max's social media, insisted that she show him her phone, and made other demands for transparency. At least two or three times per week, Eddie uncovered some other betrayal by Max, and each one hit him as hard as the first one. Even worse, Max continually swore that was it, and that she was being completely honest. She stated she was not cheating on him at all, and that any of the cheating she ever did hardly counted because she never felt any sort of emotional connection with the other men the way she feels it with Eddie.

Eddie described this process to friends and his therapist as 'death by paper cut,' noting that every time he found out some new bit of information, he learned that Max lied yet again. He says that the lies and secrets and cover-ups hurt him more than what she's done sexually. He begged Max to engage in full disclosure, and she continually refused, insisting that this time she really has told him everything.

Three days ago, Eddie got a call at work from Jeremy's wife, who told him about the now long-term, still ongoing, highly emotionally charged affair between Jeremy and Max. For Eddie, this was the final straw. For Max to not tell him about something that important, and to still be cheating on him despite her hundreds of statements to the contrary, was more than he could handle. He asked his boss for the rest of the day off, pulled his kids out of school, and took them to his mother's house. He changed the locks on the doors of their house and phoned a divorce lawyer.

Therapeutic Disclosure

Learning about intimate betrayal is incredibly traumatic, so you want to do the best job possible with disclosure. Otherwise, you risk doing more damage to the betrayed partner and the relationship. The good news here is that there is an established therapeutic process for healthy and productive disclosure, and generally both partners feel better for having gone through it. Research on disclosure suggests the vast majority of people who experienced a facilitated disclosure (approximately 92%–94%) felt that it was the right thing to do.[1,2]

Research on infidelity has shown that when the participating partner is open and fully honest during therapeutic disclosure and willingly answers the betrayed partner's questions as thoroughly and accurately as possible, there is a much greater likelihood of healing the relationship and staying together.[3] Even though disclosure may feel like a daunting process, it is the first major step in the process of healing.

Full Disclosure About Full Disclosure

There are no guarantees that disclosure will save your relationship. But if you love your partner and want to stay together, you need to re-establish trust, and that starts with full and complete disclosure of the betrayal. As full disclosure occurs, participating partners need to be realistic about the fact that their betrayed partner is likely to be extremely upset, mostly because the information is hard to hear and the betrayed partner does not want it to be true. That said, when betrayed partners see their participating partner being honest, open, and accountable, they are likely to feel, in addition to anger and other 'negative' emotions, relief about finally having all of the information and hope for the future of their relationship.

To begin the process of full disclosure, you should each find a therapist who is well-versed in relationship betrayal and therapeutic disclosure. Before agreeing to work with a therapist, you should ask the therapist directly if he or she has experience with this type of work. If the answer is no, look for a different therapist to do your disclosure process. The therapists listed on iitap.com or sexhelp.com are well trained in the process of therapeutic disclosure. Those websites also provide information about treatment centers that will perform therapeutic disclosures in an intensive format.

Case History: James and Stuart

James and Stuart have been together for a little over ten years. They have not gotten married, but they both say they treat their relationship as if they are. James is, by nature, traditional in many respects, especially with his relationship. He is and has always been monogamous. Stuart, on the other hand, has engaged in infidelity from the start.

James knows of at least two affairs Stuart has had. With one, Stuart's affair partner called James and told him, hoping to break the couple apart. With the other, the one James just recently learned about, James' doctor informed him that he had an STD, which he could only have gotten from Stuart.

In the first case, Stuart denied having an affair and said the man who called James was crazy and only *wanted* to have an affair. A few days later, after James had engaged in a bit of detective work, he confronted Stuart with hard evidence. At that point, Stuart admitted that he had hooked up with this individual, but only once, and that it would never happen again.

In the more recent case, Stuart initially tried to blame James for the STD, alleging that James must be the one cheating. At that point, James asked if he could look through Stuart's phone apps and text history. Stuart refused but did admit that he'd hooked up with someone from the gym and must have picked up the STD from him. Again, Stuart insisted that it only happened the one time, and said he had learned his lesson.

James believes that Stuart has had at least a few other affairs and that he's been hooking up on a regular basis with men he meets at the gym, on Grindr, and elsewhere. Now that he knows for sure that he's not crazy and making up stories about Stuart's actions because he's jealous, paranoid, suffering from anxiety, or any of a dozen other 'issues,' as Stuart has accused him of over the years, he has demanded the truth, repeatedly asking to know everything.

Stuart is distressed and worried that James will end their relationship because of his cheating. He has agreed to go to therapy to help him deal with what he believes is sexual addiction. He does not, however, want to 'come clean' about his years of infidelity because he thinks that if James knows everything, it will hurt him too badly.

Meanwhile, James, who is also seeing a therapist to help him cope with his feelings and his post-traumatic stress response to the betrayal, continues to desire and ask for the complete truth. He says that neither he nor the relationship can heal until he knows that Stuart is finally being honest with him.

After several weeks of back and forth, guidance from their individual therapists, and direction toward disclosure from an experienced couples therapist, Stuart has finally agreed to provide therapeutic disclosure. James has presented him with a list of questions, and Stuart is preparing a 'formal disclosure document' that he will share with James in a joint therapy session. Stuart has also agreed to take a polygraph test after the disclosure so James will know that he finally has all of the information.

Both Stuart and James are worried about disclosure. James is worried about what he might learn. Stuart is worried about how James will respond. Both are worried that their relationship might not survive the truth. However, both men are relieved that full disclosure will take place. James says he already feels better about his relationship because he knows he's finally going to get the whole truth and that he can then make intelligent decisions based on that. Stuart says he's already feeling better about himself because, with full disclosure, he knows that he finally can stop living a stressful double life.

Preparing for Disclosure

The next section is mostly directed towards the participating partner who will be preparing their disclosure statement. However, betrayed partners should read this section so they know what to expect.

There are some important guidelines to keep in mind while preparing to give a formal disclosure. First and foremost, you should only give this type of disclosure if you and your betrayed partner are working toward rebuilding trust and saving your relationship. If you are in the process of ending your relationship, full disclosure could do both of you more harm than good. That said, the fact that you're reading this book is a pretty good indication that you want and need to engage in the process of full disclosure.

It is also important to keep in mind that there are no guarantees that participating in a full disclosure will save your relationship. Some betrayed partners will learn information that they will perceive as an insurmountable betrayal and they may decide to leave the relationship. But in many cases, when betrayed partners see they are finally getting the full truth with genuine accountability and remorse, they paradoxically feel enough hope to continue and re-invest in the relationship. Unfortunately, there's no way to predict their response prior to doing a full disclosure.

Preparing to present full disclosure is a very structured process. Participating partners, your therapist will review your disclosure document, give you important feedback, and prepare you to give disclosure. A second therapist will do similar work with your betrayed partner. Preparation for disclosure is done separately so each partner has the emotional and psychological support that he or she needs.

As you prepare your disclosure document, you should be invested in and committed to your relationship. All ties to your infidelity should be severed. You should do whatever needs to be done to achieve closure in those relationships. After that, you should have no further contact with any sexual acting out partners. Those individuals should be blocked from your phone and email. If you used technology to facilitate your behavior, you should take measures to filter or disable your access to problematic websites, apps, and any other technology that was part of your betrayal.

You should do these things for two reasons:

1. Taking these measures demonstrates your commitment to yourself that you are going to do whatever it takes to save your relationship.
2. Your partner is certain to ask questions about these issues, and you want to make sure you can provide satisfactory answers.

As you are preparing for disclosure, your therapist and your partner's therapist will communicate to let you know the specific information that your partner would like to have included. If there are specific questions your partner would like you to answer, you will know about that in advance so you can address these questions in your disclosure document. You should answer all of these questions during disclosure.

It is incredibly important that you provide clear, concise, factual information in your disclosure document. This information should not in any way be vague or unclear. That said, providing information that is too detailed or graphic can increase your partner's trauma, causing an escalation in emotional volatility and other PTSD symptoms. Some betrayed partners find it hard to get images and details of the cheating out of their mind, which makes it more difficult to heal the relationship. So be careful with the language you use and the amount of detail you provide. Disclosures that are too detailed or too graphic tend to be less effective. Your therapist can provide you with guidance about how much detail should be included on your disclosure document.

Keep in mind that the goal of disclosure is clarity. This is your chance to tell the complete truth and to clear up any confusion your partner might have about your acting out. This means you must share complete information about your sexual misbehavior. Do not withhold information. If you withhold information and your partner uncovers it later, your partner will view that as yet another betrayal. After that, it will be very difficult to restore relationship trust. So you need to be completely open and honest in your disclosure.

After you share your disclosure in a joint therapy session, your partner will have the ability to ask questions, and you should be ready to answer openly and honestly. Be ready for your partner to ask the same question more than once. This is actually relatively common, and it occurs because the answers you give can be painful to hear and difficult to process.

Usually, it is a good idea to review your disclosure document with not only your therapist but others in your support network before you share it with your partner. That way, you can receive extra feedback, and your support network will fully understand what you're about to do. No matter what, you need to work with your therapist to create a support plan for yourself for the week following disclosure. Your partner will also have an extensive support plan for the week following disclosure.

The language you utilize in your disclosure document should be clear and factual with no use of slang or jargon. For example, you might say something like, "I had protected genital intercourse with our neighbor, Cindy. This occurred on approximately 20 occasions. I lied to you about this by concealing the nature of my relationship with her. When you asked me about her, I invented information to cover up the affair. All of the sexual acting out occurred in her home."

Again, the importance of this advice cannot be overstated: You need to be clear and honest without sharing information that is too detailed or graphic. Excessive and graphic details can be traumatizing for your partner. If you have questions about the level of detail to include, discuss this with your therapist before you give disclosure.

In addition to answering questions posed by your betrayed partner, your disclosure document should include:

- Types of sexual behaviors you engaged in (pornography, prostitution, affairs, strip clubs, objectification, etc.)
- A general description of the sexual activity you engaged in (protected, unprotected, oral, genital, anal, etc.)

- Timeframes for acting out
- Frequency of acting out
- If it was an affair, whether it was an emotional affair or a purely sexual affair
- If your partner knows any of your acting out partners, the names of those people
- Health information (STDs, recent test results, etc.)
- Financial information
- Legal consequences
- Lying to and keeping secrets from your partner to cover up your behavior
- Accountability language where you take responsibility for your behavior

Disclosure Preparation Worksheet

The following worksheet provides you with guidance about what should be included in your disclosure. As you complete the worksheet and write your disclosure document, please do not leave your paperwork in a place where your betrayed partner might find it. It is important that he or she hears this information in a supportive, therapist-facilitated environment, and that it comes from you directly.

Use the following table to compile a list of the information to be included in your disclosure document.

Sample Worksheet: Summary of Information to Disclose

Type of Behavior	Timeframe and Frequency	Location	Description	Cost	How Did I Hide This?
Pornography	2–3 times per week, each session lasting approximately 1 hour	My home office	My use of pornography involved consenting adults. Common themes included lesbian sex, threesomes, and S/M (pain exchange).	I used free pornography websites, so the cost included wasted time, when I could have been doing something financially productive.	I lied about what I was doing, deleted my history on my computer, and used my phone in private mode. When caught, I minimized and normalized my behavior.
Sexual Affair	June 2018 to May 2019. This included approximately 20 sexual encounters and flirtation via email and text.	I often texted and sexted from work and from my office at home. All encounters occurred at her house.	This sexual affair involved sexting, flirtation, and intrigue using my phone. On approximately 20 occasions I had protected genital intercourse with this affair partner. This was a sexual affair, not emotional.	This affair did not cost me anything financially other than lost time and productivity. I did not purchase dinner or gifts for this partner.	I always hid my phone to cover up my sexting and texting. I used fictitious work engagements to hide my whereabouts during this affair.
Camming	This behavior began in 2013. I did this about 1 time per week, each session lasting approximately 1 hour.	I often did this in my home office after you went to bed.	My pornography use escalated to using webcam sites. This involved paying for webcam sessions with women who would perform sex acts for me online.	I spent approximately $300 per month on camming sites. This behavior has been occurring for the past six years for a total cost of approximately $22,000.	I always made sure to pay with credit cards to hide it. I would do this on 'private' mode on my phone to hide it.

Your Worksheet: Summary of Information to Disclose

Type of Behavior	Timeframe and Frequency	Location	Description	Cost	How Did I Hide This?

Type of Behavior	Timeframe and Frequency	Location	Description	Cost	How Did I Hide This?

Type of Behavior	Timeframe and Frequency	Location	Description	Cost	How Did I Hide This?

Creating Your Disclosure Document

Now that you have compiled all the relevant information, you need to organize that information in a clear, concise, and logical manner. Use the following five-section guide as the framework for your disclosure document.

Section 1: Purpose

Make a statement about the purpose and intent of doing your disclosure. Your partner will want to know why you are making this disclosure and what you would like to achieve. Keep this section succinct and to the point. An overly ingratiating plea may be received by your partner as an attempt to manipulate his or her response. Finish this section by asking your partner if he or she is ready and willing to hear what you have to say.

> Example:
> I am doing this disclosure with you today to be honest with you about my sexual behaviors. I want to make sure I have cleared up any questions you have about my betrayals to our relationship. My intention is to be completely honest and accountable, and to answer any questions you might have. Ultimately, my long-term goal is to re-establish trust and to repair the damage I have done to our relationship. Are you ready and willing to hear my disclosure?

Section 2: Brief Summary of Behaviors that Pre-Dated the Relationship

List cheating and sexually acting out behaviors that pre-dated your relationship. You do not need to share about these behaviors in detail. Simply provide a list and a brief explanation. The purpose of this is to provide context so your betrayed partner can know if this type of behavior occurred before you met and can see if this has been a long-standing pattern. You can provide more information in this section if you think it might help your partner make sense of how your behavior progressed over time. If you had no cheating or sexually addictive behavior that pre-dated your relationship, simply skip this section.

Example:

My behavior started well before I met you. It has been steadily progressing and escalating. It began when I discovered pornography at age 12. I learned at that point that pornography could be used to escape and numb my feelings. My pornography use escalated to strip clubs and prostitution when I went away to college. And just prior to when we met, I was actively using hookup apps for casual sex. During many of my previous relationships, I had affairs. In summary, prior to meeting you, my behaviors included the following:

- Pornography
- Objectifying
- Affairs
- Casual sex
- Strip clubs
- Prostitution

Section 3: Description of Betrayal Events

Describe the behaviors you engaged in after the start of your current relationship. It is helpful if these are listed in an organized fashion, which usually means chronological order.

As you write out the information, it is important that you demonstrate accountability. This includes owning the deception and the lies surrounding your behavior in addition to owning the behavior itself. Use clear facts with enough detail to not leave your partner guessing about important aspects of your behavior. If you have questions about whether something should be included, seek the guidance of your therapist.

You may want to include some background information about what was occurring in your life at the time you cheated, to provide context that could help your partner make sense of the timeline. Be as complete as possible. Be sure to include all of the cheating behaviors and events on your worksheet.

Example #1:

Shortly after we moved to California, my pornography use escalated. During that time, you were pregnant with Brandon. I rationalized my behavior and made excuses that you probably wouldn't be interested in sex anyway, and then I made no attempts to seek intimacy with you. Instead, I lied about my behavior and concealed it. I used pornography to medicate my anxiety about the pregnancy, and even though you made regular attempts to connect with me physically and emotionally, I withdrew into my sexual addiction. My behavior escalated and eventually I was using pornography about 10 hours per week, sometimes more than that. The sites I frequented included consenting adults. The themes I visited frequently included sadomasochistic behavior and group sex. I was never open about my interest in these behaviors with you. I hid that part of my sexuality from you.

Example #2

After I got my job at the airline, I was traveling for work and away from home frequently. I used this as an opportunity to act out sexually. Two months after I started working there, I met Jim, who you know, and began an ongoing sexual affair with him. This affair began in June of 2017 and ended in November of 2017, just before Thanksgiving. Jim was on my route whenever I did trips to New York, which was about twice per month. During these trips, after the flight, we usually had sex in one of our hotel rooms. This included oral and genital unprotected sex. I drank during these occasions to medicate my guilt, and this escalated my drinking. I lied to you and deceived you about my activities on these trips. There were times when you were suspicious of my behavior and I manipulated you by denying your justifiable suspicions. The affair with Jim ended when his wife discovered it. He changed routes, and I no longer have contact with him.

Section 4: Cost Estimate Summary

Include a summary of money spent during your sexual infidelity. Use the worksheet you completed earlier to summarize all costs associated with your cheating. If the costs are extensive, you may want to utilize a spreadsheet. Be sure to explain how you came up with the number.

Examples:

- Prostitutes—2 times per month @ $300 each over 10 years = $72,000
- Strip clubs—4 times per month @ $150 each visit over 5 years = $36,000
- Gifts for affair partner = $4,500

Section 5: Permission for Boundaries and Self-Care, and Closing

Your betrayed partner will likely need some time to digest and process the information you disclose. He or she will likely be extremely upset and want some time apart to think. Let your partner know that you understand that he or she will need some time to make sense out of what he or she just heard and to decide on healthy boundaries. Make a statement that lets your partner know you will honor his or her need for boundaries and self-care. Close with a statement about your commitment to working on the relationship. Be careful to not ask for forgiveness, be manipulative, or try to gain sympathy.

Example:

I know that this disclosure was probably very difficult for you to hear and that you may need some time to process and think about what I have shared. I understand that you may have some boundaries you need to set, and I'm willing and open to hearing about those. I understand that you may need some time to take care of yourself and think about what my actions mean for our relationship. I want you to know that I will do anything I can to support your needs during this time. I want you to know that I am willing to work hard to recover and to repair our relationship.

Sample Rules for a Full Disclosure Session

1. All parties will maintain a tone of respect during the disclosure process. If either party gets abusive, the session will be paused and then resumed when both parties can be respectful.
2. There will be no audio recording of the session.
3. Either party can ask for a break during the session if necessary.
4. Both parties should try to maintain eye contact and stay emotionally present as much as possible.

5. When the betrayed partner asks questions, those questions will be "clarifying" questions about the addictive behavior. Questions about the meaning of the behavior or any feelings associated with the behavior will be processed during a subsequent session.
6. Both parties will drive separately to and from the session, bringing a support person.
7. Both parties will follow their aftercare plan for the week.
8. After disclosure, the participating partner will give the betrayed partner space in which to process the information he/she received. It is best to keep interactions between the parties superficial until there is sufficient time to process the information disclosed.

Sample Session Format

Section 1: Orientation

The couple will come together at the appointed time and the therapists will check in with both parties to make sure everyone is ready, willing, and able to proceed with the disclosure. The format and ground rules of the session will be reviewed.

Step 2: Disclosure Sharing

The participating partner will read his/her document in its entirety to the betrayed partner. The betrayed partner can write down questions that he/she may have. The betrayed partner may slow down the session at any time or ask for information to be repeated.

Step 3: Break To Meet With Individual Therapists

The session will pause and both parties will meet with their individual therapist. The betrayed partner and his/her therapist will review the disclosure document together. The betrayed partner will write down any clarifying questions, and his/her therapist will provide grounding as needed. The participating partner's therapist will provide support to him/her as needed.

Step 4: Questions and Clarification

The betrayed partner will ask the participating partner any additional questions that he/she has. The participating partner will answer those questions as honestly as possible.

Step 5: Wrap-Up
The therapists will check in with both parties. Aftercare plans will be revisited.

Sample Disclosure Letter

Dear Sam,

My goal for this meeting is to be completely open and honest about all my past sexual betrayals. I know that this is the right thing to do for our relationship and also for my recovery. I am willing to answer any questions you might have about any of my past behaviors. I am committed to being 100 percent honest. I am also 100 percent committed to my recovery and to working on our relationship.

Are you ready and willing to hear my disclosure?

My behaviors started before we met. I remember as a little girl using sex as a way to detract from painful feelings and get attention from men. I often used it as a validation of my worth as a person. When I became a teenager, I used sex as a way to medicate painful feelings and soothe my insecurities. During my teenage years I was very sexually promiscuous. I went from one relationship to another, often starting new relationships before old ones ended. I developed a pattern of infidelity, and that developed into sexual obsession. These obsessions distracted me from the pain of my life and became a long-standing pattern. When I was about 14, I began to masturbate compulsively. I used masturbation to reduce anxiety. I denied the fact that I was using sex to get validation and was unaware of the fact that I used it to medicate. I also minimized its impact on me and others, including you, by telling myself that I just enjoyed "casual sex" and had a "high sex drive." When sex apps like Tinder became popular, I used them frequently and normalized my behavior by telling myself I was normal for my generation. I did that even though deep inside I knew there was something that was not healthy about my sexual behavior.

Prior to meeting you, I engaged in the following behaviors:

- *Pornography*

- *Compulsive masturbation*

- *Affairs in previous relationships*

- *Casual sexual encounters*

- *Objectifying*

- *Lying*

- *Manipulating*

These behaviors all continued during my relationship with you. At the beginning of our relationship, I used pornography approximately three times per week. Over time, my porn use has escalated to daily use and I have always kept it hidden from you. I did that by using it on my phone, which was password protected and would have been very difficult for you to track. When you complained about my cell phone use, I lied to you by telling you I was on Facebook. I also manipulated you by telling you to get off my back and stop nagging me about it.

In addition to using porn on my phone, I used dating websites. I had profiles on several sites, and I used them to communicate with potential acting out partners. This started after we had been married about one year. Initially, it was infrequent, but over time it escalated. I did not act out with anyone until three years into our relationship (January of 2010), when I met a sex partner through one of the sites. I had a sexual affair with this man that included protected genital intercourse. It lasted six months, and he broke it off when his wife found out. There were times during this affair that you wondered about my whereabouts. I lied to you and told you I was working. Sometimes I created fake work events to hide my behavior from you. You started to complain about my working long hours. I disregarded your feelings and concerns.

After this affair, I got the Tinder app. I used this app to seek hookups with men. In the last six years, I have had sex with approximately 20 men using this app. Except as stated below, I used protection. These were casual sexual experiences that had no emotional involvement and, except as stated below, they occurred one time (one-night stands). You discovered my Tinder profile and learned I was communicating with men. You were hurt by this. I objectified these men, and I lied to you, made excuses, and minimized my behavior.

In June of 2012, when you were traveling a lot for your work with the bank, I got involved in another sexual affair with someone I met on Tinder. This sexual affair lasted approximately nine months. It included unprotected oral, genital, and anal intercourse. It was not an emotional affair. Again, I lied to you, stating that I was working, along with other excuses.

The final affair I had occurred in 2015 with Craig Denson. I met Craig through an adult dating website. The affair was sexual and included unprotected oral, genital, and anal intercourse. This affair lasted ten months. You discovered this affair when his girlfriend Denise contacted you and told you about him.

Sam, I imagine this information has been very difficult for you to hear, and I understand that you will need some time to process the new information and make sense out of it. I will give you whatever time you need, and I support whatever you need to do to take care of yourself. If you have new boundaries to share with me, I am open to hearing those. I am fully committed to doing whatever it takes to work on and repair our relationship.

Sincerely,
Andrea

Sharing Your Disclosure Letter

Typically, therapeutic disclosure is set up so each partner has his or her own therapist involved in the process, possibly with assistance from a third therapist (usually an experienced couples counselor). The therapists will create a format for the session and its aftermath. Most likely, after you read your disclosure document, your betrayed partner will have the opportunity to ask questions, and you will need to answer those questions as fully and honestly as possible.

Betrayed Partners: Your Role in Disclosure

As a betrayed partner, you will be asked by your therapist to provide a list of questions you would like answered during disclosure. Please use the worksheets below to help you understand what you want and need to know in disclosure (and, just as importantly, what you don't want or need to know). Most likely, you will give this information to your therapist, who will share it with your partner's therapist, who will share it with your partner to make sure he or she addresses all of your issues and concerns. Your therapist will also let you know if you're asking for information that might traumatize you because it is too detailed or too graphic.

What would you like to know?

....

....

....

....

....

....

....

What do you *not* want to know?

....

....

....

....

....

....

....

....

Beyond preparing your list of questions, your role in therapeutic disclosure is to listen to what your participating partner has to say, and to engage in self-care in the days and weeks that follow. Hopefully, once you've heard your partner's truth, you'll be able to accept it and you will start the process of rebuilding trust. That said, it will be many months before trust levels return to something even approaching normal.

Some betrayed partners, after hearing disclosure, find that trauma therapy is needed. If you find yourself struggling to process and move forward after disclosure, it is important that you seek this type of therapeutic assistance. There are many wonderful trauma treatments that can help you walk through your pain, including eye movement desensitization reprocessing (EMDR), somatic experiencing, sensorimotor psychotherapy, internal family systems work (IFS), post-induction therapy, psychodrama, art therapy, and more.

Hearing Your Participating Partner's Disclosure

As stated earlier, therapeutic disclosure is usually set up so each partner has his or her own therapist, with support from a third therapist (most often an experienced couples therapist). Working together, the therapists will create a format for the session and its aftermath. Typically, you will be asked to sit quietly while your partner reads his or her disclosure letter. Then you will have an opportunity to ask questions and seek clarification.

Self-Care After Disclosure

After the disclosure experience, it's likely both of you will feel emotionally raw. As such, self-care in the aftermath of disclosure is critical. It's likely that the betrayed partner's trauma symptoms will increase for a while, and he or she may experience feelings of overwhelming sadness. Participating partners usually feel things like shame, depression, and anxiety. It is likely that your therapist will ask you to create a 'safety' or 'support' plan for the week following the disclosure. Take this advice seriously. Plan out support activities throughout the week, especially in the evenings. Pay attention to your body and your emotions and ask yourself what you need at this time. Spending time with your support network, exercising, meditating, journaling, and yoga are self-care activities that you may find helpful.

After disclosure is given, the betrayed partner will need several days (or longer) to digest and process the information presented. Hopefully, you both have some extra therapy sessions scheduled—both individually and as a couple—to help with this.

Case History Continued: James and Stuart

For James and Stuart, whose case history was initially presented earlier in this chapter, therapeutic disclosure was a turning point in their relationship. It was also a turning point for Stuart in his recovery from sexual addiction. Although preparation for the disclosure process took longer than James might have liked, he was willing to be patient and trust the knowledge and guidance of the therapists involved—once he knew for sure that Stuart was preparing to disclose everything and to take a polygraph test afterward.

Working with his therapist, James prepared his rather lengthy list of questions, asking things like:

- How many people did you have sex with during our relationship?
- Did you have any longer-term affairs that I don't know about?
- Do I know any of those people? If so, who?
- How much money did you spend on these behaviors?
- How many times did you have unprotected sex while acting out?
- Are you willing to install filtering/monitoring/tracking software on your digital devices?

Stuart used these and other questions posed by James, along with the guidelines listed above, as the basis for his disclosure. He told his therapist, when he got the list of questions from James, "I guess he probably knows or has guessed a lot more than I thought." He also said he was grateful to be taking a polygraph after disclosure because that was going to force him to include everything. Even though he dreaded doing that, he knew it was best for his recovery and best for his relationship.

The formal disclosure session was led by their individual therapists in a conjoint session. Both men had self-care plans in place for after the session. Stuart made it clear that he felt terrible about hurting James and was willing to do whatever was needed to help James heal and to repair their relationship. Then he talked about how he'd been acting out sexually since his early teens as a way of coping with his dysfunctional home life and his internalized shame about being gay, and how many of his acting out behaviors continued into adulthood and his relationship with James. He took responsibility for the betrayal and his recovery from sexual addiction, and let James know he would respect any boundaries James needed to implement to feel safe.

At that point, there was a break in the session so both men could process what was disclosed and James could formulate additional questions. Then everyone came back together. James asked for clarification on one issue, Stuart answered, and James presented some boundaries he wanted Stuart to follow. Stuart agreed to follow those boundaries and to return the next day for a polygraph exam to confirm he'd told the entire truth in his disclosure statement.

The days and weeks following disclosure were not easy, as there was a lot for James to feel angry about, and a lot for Stuart to feel guilty about. But both men agreed that with everything out in the open, there was a much better chance for both individual and relationship healing. Each man realized how much he loved the other, and how much he wanted to stay together despite the betrayal. Both men were glad they'd engaged in a process of therapeutic disclosure.

CHAPTER THREE:

Sharing, Listening, and Grieving

One of the main causes of couples failing to heal after a painful betrayal is that they don't effectively communicate about the feelings and pain the betrayal has caused. Without appropriate expression of this pain, the wound can fester.

The good news is that deep emotional sharing about the pain can clean out that wound. However, this is one of the most difficult parts of the healing process. And betrayed partners, this work falls squarely on your shoulders. Now that you have heard your participating partner's disclosure and understand the total nature of the betrayal, you need to identify and share in a comprehensive manner about how the betrayal has impacted you.

You can do this with an impact letter. With an impact letter, you write down your feelings about the betrayal, and then you share that with your participating partner. The goal of sharing an impact letter is that it provides an opportunity for partners to share, in a deep and profound way, the pain caused by the betrayal. In the impact letter the partner highlights the significant pain points and expresses to the participating partner in detail how this has impacted them. This provides a chance for the participating partner to truly "get it" and understand how much their behavior has hurt them. This is a significant step in the healing process. It may take many sessions with your therapist, often your couples therapist, to share and process the impact letter. Some impact letters can be lengthy, as it is important that they be comprehensive and address all the key pain points surrounding the betrayal.

Most betrayed partners find that being honest in such a profound and meaningful way helps them feel like they're getting a weight off their chest. They also feel empowered as they give voice to their hurt, pain, and suffering.

As you write your impact letter, use the worksheets provided below, which are designed to help you gather your thoughts together.

Participating partners, your betrayed partner may need some extra support while he or she is working on an impact letter. Do everything you can to be there for your betrayed partner. If your partner needs privacy or space, provide that. If your partner needs quiet time, help to create that. If your partner needs help with chores that he or she normally handles so he or she can focus on writing the impact letter, step in and take care of those tasks.

Case Example: Melissa and Larry

Melissa and Larry are in their early 50s. They've been together for a little more than ten years, each after a messy divorce – Melissa's precipitated by her husband's cheating; Larry's precipitated by his wife's alcoholism. Because of their previous experience with marriage and divorce, they have decided to live together without getting married; but as part of that agreement, they've agreed to be monogamous.

About three months ago, Melissa found evidence of porn on Larry's laptop computer. When she confronted him about it, he blamed his 25-year-old son, and together he and Melissa deleted all the evidence and wiped the browser history. Melissa made it clear that looking at porn was not part of their relationship agreement, and Larry agreed. Then, about two months later, Melissa again found evidence of porn. This time, she was not willing to hear any excuses about Larry's son, especially since he'd been out of town for several months.

At this point, Melissa pressed Larry to tell her about anything else he'd been doing. She knew from experience with her first husband that she would not be able to heal herself or the relationship without the full truth. Larry insisted there was nothing else to know. He'd looked at porn a few times and was sorry. He said it wouldn't happen again. Melissa would not let it go, though, and finally, after several weeks, Larry owned up to the fact that it was not only porn. He went to strip clubs on numerous occasions as well. Melissa was overwhelmed, had no support network in place, and was unable to process her feelings.

For the last week, Melissa has been self-medicating with wine. With Larry, she alternates between screaming at him and apologizing for being drunk. Both Melissa and Larry say they love each other and want to heal the relationship, but neither is sure that is possible. They've agreed to enter couples counseling, but neither is hopeful. Too many old scabs have been ripped off. Their therapist is hopeful that since Melissa now knows everything, the process of healing can begin with an impact preparation letter.

Impact Letter Preparation Worksheets

As a betrayed partner, you will need to collect your thoughts before you write your impact letter. The following worksheets will help you do this. First, you need to evaluate the areas of life in which you have experienced pain, mistrust, and consequences. Next you will look at lies, deception, and gaslighting. You will also look at self-blame, sexuality, and broken promises and vows.

As you complete the following worksheets, consider the following questions:

- Have you had health consequences, such as illnesses or STDs?
- Have you had consequences to your friendships? For example, have you lost friendships due to your partner's acting out, or withdrawn into isolation because you didn't want to tell people what was happening in your life?
- Do you worry that your relationship with your partner will never be the same?
- Have you experienced financial consequences, perhaps related to job loss (your own or your partner's) or money your partner spent while cheating? Are there now additional costs for treatment?
- Have you experienced psychological consequences, such as shame, low self-esteem, depression, anxiety, PTSD symptoms, and the like?
- Have you experienced spiritual consequences, possibly a loss of faith or an existential crisis (wondering what is the meaning of all of this)?
- Have you experienced sexual consequences, such as a lack of desire, feelings of disgust, or a lack of intimacy?

- Has the betrayal impacted your ability to function at work or at home? If so, in what ways?
- How have your children been impacted? Have they learned information that will be traumatic for them? Have they experienced tension and conflict in the home?

Analysis of Consequences

Type of Consequence	Description	Thoughts	Feelings
Health Consequences			
Friendship/Relationship Consequences			

Type of Consequence	Description	Thoughts	Feelings
Financial Consequences			
Psychological Consequences			
Spiritual Consequences			

Type of Consequence	Description	Thoughts	Feelings
Sexual Consequences			
Professional Consequences			
Consequences to Your Children			

Analysis of Lies, Deception, and Gaslighting

In addition to the consequences listed above, you've also experienced a loss of relationship trust. In all likelihood, you now question everything your partner says and does. If so, it's because of the lies, deception, and gaslighting that he or she engaged in as part of the addiction.

In the space below, make a list of all the lies that your participating partner told you. Be specific. After each lie, write how you felt when you heard it (i.e., confused, angry, afraid, ashamed, etc.)

1. ....

2. ....

3. ....

....

....

....

....

....

....

....

....

....

....

....

....

....

Self-Blame

Have there been moments when you blamed yourself for the participating partner's behavior? If so, list those moments, along with your thoughts about those moments now.

....

....

....

....

....

....

....

....

....

....

....

....

....

....

Sexuality

After hearing your participating partner's disclosure, you may have feelings about the specific behaviors that he or she participated in. List your participating partner's sexual behaviors and your thoughts and feelings about these.

Your Partner's Sexual Behavior	Your Thoughts	Your Feelings

Your Partner's Sexual Behavior	Your Thoughts	Your Feelings

Broken Promises and Vows

In the following section, make a list of the broken promises and vows that were made to you by your participating partner and your thoughts and feelings about each of those.

Broken Promise/Vow	Your Thoughts	Your Feelings

Broken Promise/Vow	Your Thoughts	Your Feelings

Betrayed Partners: Impact Letter

Once you have completed the worksheets above and evaluated important areas of impact, you are ready to write a letter communicating your pain to your participating partner. This letter outlines in detail how the betrayal has affected you. Since the letter is meant to be comprehensive, it can be lengthy. The point is to help your participating partner understand your pain. You want your partner to truly comprehend your experience and to understand how deeply you've been hurt.

As you write your letter, keep the following suggestions in mind:

- Be specific and offer personal examples of your experiences.
- Be willing to describe your feelings, no matter how painful.
- Though your impact letter is an expression of your pain, avoid blaming, shaming, or berating your participating partner.
- Since writing the letter can be a highly emotional experience, do this exercise with the support of a therapist.

Below are guidelines for writing your letter. Include as many of the suggested elements as you can. Please review your letter with your therapist, support group, or sponsor before sharing it with your partner.

Section 1: Evaluation of the Disclosure Process

In this section, describe how the unfolding disclosure process has impacted you. Did you initially make discoveries on your own? Did your participating partner share information about the betrayal in little pieces over time? How did you feel when you discovered each new bit of information? How did this affect your emotional stability? Was it staggered disclosure and was it traumatic for you? Was there information that was particularly disappointing or emotional for you? Share specific incidents that were particularly painful. If you received a therapeutic disclosure, what was that like? Paint a picture of your emotional experience. What were the most painful aspects of this?

Section 2: Description of Consequences

In this section, describe how the betrayal has impacted all areas of your life. Explain in detail the consequences you've experienced because of your partner's behavior. Describe the physical, relational, psychological, financial, sexual, and professional consequences you've had. Also describe any consequences to your children.

Section 3: Evaluation of the Lies, Deception, and Gaslighting

In this section, describe how your partner's deception has impacted you. Identify ways your partner was intentionally deceptive and manipulative. Describe specific examples of 'crazy-making' behavior and how you feel about them. Did the deception cause you to doubt yourself? What has it been like to learn the truth and realize the extent of the lies? How has it been to reclaim your reality around this truth?

Section 4: Self-Blame

You may have found yourself mistakenly blaming yourself for your partner's behavior. For example, you might have thought that if you had been a more available lover, less angry, more loving, etc., then maybe this wouldn't have happened. It is important for you to realize that you are not to blame for the sexual betrayal. In this section, tell your partner what your struggles were in this area and how his or her deceit caused you to doubt yourself. Explain to your partner that you realize now that you are not and never were at fault. Describe how you feel about thinking that you were. Use your voice to empower yourself, and to divest yourself of responsibility for the betrayal.

Section 5: Sexuality

Describe your thoughts and feelings about your partner's sexual behaviors. When you discovered what he or she was doing—for example, seeing prostitutes, having sex with someone in your bed, using pornography—what feelings came up for you? Are there particular behaviors that trouble you? What has it been like for you to learn about this aspect of your partner's sexuality?

Describe how your partner's behaviors have affected your own sexuality. How has the betrayal changed your sexual relationship with your partner? How about your individual sexuality? Do you feel concerns about your body or your sexual functioning? Has this impaired your sexual functioning?

Section 6: Fear and Shame

Describe any fears you have about others judging you, judging your partner, or judging your relationship. Do you feel shame and embarrassment about your partner's behavior? Have you experienced public embarrassment related to the behavior? If so, how has this affected you? When you think about other people who know about the betrayal or who might find out, what thoughts come to your mind?

Section 7: Impact on the Relationship

Describe how the betrayal has impacted your relationship. Have you lost the feelings of safety and connection you once had? Does your knowledge of the betrayal and deception affect your ability to trust in the relationship? What promises or vows that your partner made to you have been broken? How do you feel about trusting your partner going forward? Do you feel that trust can be restored? What will you need to see and experience for that to happen?

Section 8: Boundaries

In this section, outline briefly what you will do to take care of yourself as you move forward after formal disclosure. Are there new boundaries you will need to put in place to protect yourself? Consider your emotional, physical, and sexual needs at this time. Are there any boundaries relating to your children, friends, or family that you need to implement? Outline any other special needs you have at this time.

Section 9: Closing

Close by acknowledging that this letter will likely be hard for your partner to hear. Let your partner know that the purpose of this letter was to share your feelings about the addiction and your relationship moving forward. Thank your partner for reading or hearing the letter.

> **Note to Betrayed Partners**
>
> The following letter is a brief sample. Some impact letters are short like this one. Others can be long, and may take several therapy sessions to share with your partner. You write your letter in a way that feels right for you.

Sample Impact Letter

Dear Ron,

I am writing this letter so you will have a better understanding of how your infidelity over the course of our marriage has affected me. My hope is that if you hear my feelings about your behavior, especially the lies, secrets, and manipulation, you will 'get it' as far as why I'm angry one minute, afraid the next, and happy the next. My deepest hope is that you will finally feel some empathy for what I've experienced and what I continue to experience in our marriage.

For me, the worst of what you did was the covering up. The lies, the secrets, the gaslighting, and the partial admissions. In the beginning, when I told you I was worried, you told me I was imagining things. When I confronted you with actual evidence, you denied it and accused me of making things up. When you finally did admit to certain things, you denied everything else and blamed me for the things to which you admitted. I continually felt betrayed and abused. Sometimes I felt sick to my stomach. And the fact that several times you told me I knew everything and there was nothing more to know, but then I found out that was not true, made all of this worse. The months of staggered disclosure made it impossible for me to trust you and even to trust myself. Even after therapeutic disclosure, I find it hard to trust that you've finally told me everything.

My emotional state was a mess from the moment I first suspected you might be cheating. And when I started to see evidence that confirmed my suspicions, I was all over the place. One minute I thought it couldn't be true, the next I couldn't understand how the one person in the world who is supposed to have my back could betray me. This rollercoaster continues today, and I hate it. I feel like the fact that I can't control my emotions is my fault, and blaming myself in this way feels like yet another injury that you've perpetrated on me.

Your sexual addiction and betrayal have affected every aspect of my life. I'm short-tempered with the kids and they don't know why. I'm worried they think they're the ones who've done something wrong. That is incredibly unfair to them. I also worry about all the money you spent on your addiction, and all the money we're spending now on your recovery and on healing our damaged relationship. Worst of all, I feel like I'm so obsessed with the betrayal that I can't focus on life. Our home does not look the way it once did, the meals I serve are not as good as they used to be, and sometimes I just plain forget to do things, which never happened before the betrayal.

When you were having the affair with Janet, I knew about it, but you repeatedly told me it was over. And then you would get angry with me and tell me if I wasn't such a nag, you wouldn't need other women for support. You also said horrible things about my looks. You made me feel small and unworthy. You made me feel as if I didn't have a right to be angry. You engaged in the same belittling behaviors when I confronted you about your porn use, the hookup apps on your phone, and other indicators that you were cheating. You put me down and you kept me confused to keep me in our marriage and make me feel like our problems were all my fault, even though you were the one cheating.

The times when you just flat out lied to me and told me my mind was playing tricks on me, despite plenty of evidence you really were cheating, I wanted to believe you. I tried to believe you. But this did not mesh with reality as I was experiencing it. Sometimes I thought I was going crazy. I didn't know what was real and what wasn't.

The worst part of your betrayal was that I started to blame myself. I thought maybe I wasn't attractive enough, or loving enough, or a good enough wife, and that's why you did what you did. It ruined my self-esteem. When I knew you were using porn, I tried to lose weight and dress differently because I thought I was too fat and had let myself go. I starved myself and got horrible headaches, and I was filled with anxiety about my appearance.

Before the betrayal, I truly believed we had an ideal marriage—a nice house, great kids, and enough money to live comfortably. That's all I ever wanted. But then I found out it was all a lie. I feel like we've forever lost the marriage and life I thought we had. I feel like our life together is forever divided into before the cheating and after the cheating, and I will never be able to trust you the way I did before, that I will never be as comfortable in our relationship as I once was, that I will never be able to enjoy sex with you the way I once did, that I will never feel as comfortable with my own sexuality as I once did. I will always wonder, when we're together sexually, if you're really 'there' or if your mind is thinking about someone else.

I feel tremendous shame about what happened, like I somehow failed as a wife. And I worry about what other people know or suspect. I find myself lying to my family and yours because I don't want my family to judge me for staying with you, or your family to judge me for somehow causing you to behave this way. I've also been keeping secrets from my friends because I don't want them to know what happened, even though I know they will support me. Feeling like I need to be dishonest in this way is harming my self-esteem and sense of self. I've always prided myself on my honesty, and now I can't. I feel like I'm lying, keeping secrets, and manipulating the same as you, and that really bothers me because your lies, secrets, and manipulation hurt me and our relationship more than the actual sex behaviors you engaged in.

Your betrayal has ruined my ability to trust anything you've ever said or done. Did you ever really love me? Did you ever really care about me? It has also ruined my ability to trust others. It's not just you that I struggle to trust; it's everyone. And the fact that you continually told me bits and pieces of the story, without ever getting fully honest until formal therapeutic disclosure, made everything worse. It hurt more and more every time I found out about something else that you did. It's like you were poking a bruise. And now the pain of that bruise is affecting all my relationships.

My hope is that over time you will establish solid sexual sobriety and we will rebuild trust in our relationship. For that to happen, you will need to be diligent in your recovery and honest not only with me but with everyone in all aspects of your life. I need to know that you are going to therapy and 12-step meetings, and that you are doing the work required. If you slip up and fail to be honest with me, I need you to come clean about that within 24 hours.

I also need you to accept that I'm riding an emotional rollercoaster and it's not my fault. I need you to develop some empathy for what I've experienced and continue to experience. I need you to not blame me or get angry with me when my emotions are out of control.

I know that we will never have the relationship we had before your cheating, but maybe we can have something different that ultimately is better, more intimate, and longer-lasting. I am encouraged by the steps you have taken to overcome your addiction and repair our relationship. I also feel good about the healing work I'm doing. I want to love and respect you with all my heart and I want you to do the same for me. If we can both do that, we will not only survive, we will thrive.

Love,
Marie

When your impact letter is complete, you will need to share it with your participating partner. This should be done with the support of your therapist(s), preferably in a joint session with your therapist, your partner's therapist, or together with your couples therapist. These professionals can provide you and your partner with important feedback and much-needed support. Plus, having additional witnesses to your pain and sorrow can be healing.

Participating partners, please understand that listening to this letter will likely be the most difficult part of the healing process for you—even more difficult than presenting formal therapeutic disclosure. It is important that you recognize your partner's letter as an integral part of healing and recovery. Your betrayed partner *needs* you to understand his or her pain in order to heal, and you need to understand your partner's pain to fully recover. So please try to stay emotionally present and attuned to your partner, no matter how difficult that turns out to be.

In all likelihood, you and your partner will both shed tears as the impact letter is read. If so, let them flow. Tears are a good thing. They can wash away the sorrow and provide a platform for healing.

CHAPTER FOUR:

Emotional Restitution and Amends

Emotional Restitution

Participating partners, you just witnessed and heard your betrayed partner express deep pain around your behavior. Now it's time for you to make emotional restitution. The process of making emotional restitution involves a formal written response to your betrayed partner's impact letter, followed with actions to back that up. The goal here is to let your partner know that you understand the depths of his or her pain, to express remorse, and to demonstrate accountability for your actions and a willingness to change.

It is important that throughout your emotional restitution letter that you maintain an attitude of taking responsibility for your behavior. It is also important that you take the time to be thorough, and that you put a lot of effort into showing your partner that you truly understand the harms done, that you take your personal and relationship healing incredibly seriously, and that you intend for betrayal to never happen again.

Here are some important guidelines for writing this letter:

- Respond to the specific examples outlined in your betrayed partner's impact letter. Focus on and specifically address the areas that your partner cited as being the most painful and important.

- Do not share any new information about your acting out behavior. All information should have been shared in your formal therapeutic disclosure. If there is any new information, it should be done as an addendum to your disclosure with the support of therapists.
- Share your feelings in a truthful and genuine manner. Your betrayed partner needs to know how his or her impact letter has affected you.
- Get support while writing your letter. Share and get feedback on your letter from your therapist and sponsor before sharing it with your betrayed partner.
- After sharing your emotional restitution letter with your betrayed partner, keep in mind that it will take time for your partner to absorb and process this information. Give your partner some space. Understand that he or she might need to see that the changes you are making will stand the test of time before forgiving you and trusting you again.

In a general way, your emotional restitution letter should follow the outline of your betrayed partner's impact letter. Take time to read and re-read your partner's impact letter before you respond. It may be helpful to cover the following topics when responding.

Note to Betrayed Partners: Please keep in mind it may be difficult for your participating partner to work on this letter. Please give your partner space and quiet time if that is needed, and offer your support in any way that you can.

Topic 1: The Impact of Disclosure

Reflect on your betrayed partner's experience of the disclosure process. Validate your partner's reality around disclosure and take ownership of the pain you caused. Try to put yourself in your partner's shoes by imagining how he or she felt during this time. Respond with empathy. Normalize your partner's trauma responses to the disclosure process. Acknowledge and own any manipulations that may have occurred during the disclosure process and any attempts you made to minimize your role in your cheating behaviors.

Topic 2: Validation of Betrayed Partner Consequences

In your betrayed partner's impact letter, he or she discussed the different areas of life that were impacted by your betrayal and the consequences he or she experienced, such as physical health consequences, psychological consequences, spiritual consequences, sexual consequences, professional consequences, and consequences to the children (if applicable). Take time to reflect on those areas of life and what that must have been like for your partner. Respond to the specific losses your partner experienced and reflect on how difficult this must have been for your partner. Share what it was like for you to watch your partner experience those losses as a result of your behavior and your betrayal.

Topic 3: Validation of Your Deception

For your betrayed partner, the deception related to your betrayal was likely the most painful aspect of your behavior. Your lies and secrets destroyed relationship trust and carved a deep wound in the heart of your partner. In your betrayed partner's impact letter, he or she identified the most painful and destructive lies that you told during the betrayal. In this section, take ownership and accountability for that destructive behavior. Validate how confusing this must have been for your partner. Try to reflect on what this must have been like and provide empathy. Explain ways that you tried to confuse or gaslight your partner. Take ownership of these selfish and harmful behaviors.

Topic 4: Validation that Your Partner is Not to Blame

It is normal for betrayed partners to believe they are somehow at fault for the betrayal. They may feel as if they weren't attractive enough or sexy enough, or they did something to push you, the participating partner, into betrayal. This is often compounded by your attempts to shift the blame for your choices onto your partner. As such, it is important for you to take full responsibility for your betrayal. Taking responsibility does not mean you're at fault for all the problems in your relationship; it means that you are responsible for the betrayal. It also means that you understand you need to work on healing the betrayal before you and your betrayed partner address any other relationship issues.

Let your betrayed partner know there was nothing he or she did or didn't do that caused your actions. If you have a sex or pornography addiction, it is often helpful to provide a brief explanation of what you feel did contribute to the development of your addiction (such as early exposure to pornography, unresolved early-life trauma and abuse, etc.) It is important that you do not make these contributing factors sound like an excuse for your behavior; accountability language is crucial here. If you do refer to your trauma history and other underlying issues, it's important to remember that this is not about portraying yourself as a victim; it's about explaining that your betrayal had nothing to do with your partner.

Topic 5: Validation of Damage to Your Partner's Sexuality

Betrayal can interfere with the most sacred part of your partner, his or her sense of self and sexuality. After learning of your behavior, your betrayed partner likely has many doubts about what that means for sexual intimacy between the two of you. Your partner may have PTSD images of your behavior in his or her mind, and these images may cause your partner to feel insecure and to experience body image issues.

Your betrayed partner may also feel that now that you're both trying to heal and stay together, he or she is obligated to have sex with you—despite feeling unaroused (at least initially) by the thought of being sexual with you. It is important, as the participating partner, that you understand that when relationship trust is broken, that loss of trust can interfere with your betrayed partner's feelings of attraction toward you, and his or her feelings about sex in general. If your betrayed partner seems uninterested in sex at this time, you need to let him or her know that's okay, and you're willing to wait until trust is restored and he or she starts to once again feel an attraction toward you.

Every betrayed partner is unique and different in his or her responses. Take a moment to reflect on how your betrayal has impacted your partner's sexuality. What feelings come up for you, knowing that you have wounded this part of your partner? Try to express your feelings with compassion and understanding. Respond to the specific issues your partner raised in his or her impact letter regarding this issue. State how you commit to supporting your partner around this. It is important that you express your willingness to work on this and to be patient with whatever your betrayed partner needs.

Topic 6: Validation of Feelings of Shame and Embarrassment

Your betrayed partner may fear that people are judging him or her for staying with you, or that they're making assumptions about your relationship based on the betrayal. This type of public embarrassment, whether it's real or simply perceived, can be extremely upsetting. Reflect on what this must be like for your partner. When you think about the embarrassment, shame, and fear you have caused your partner, what thoughts come to mind for you? Validate your partner's pain and share your experiences with this same issue. Again, take full accountability for bringing this pain to your partner and to your relationship.

Topic 7: Validate the Impact of the Betrayal on Your Relationship

Your relationship as you and your betrayed partner knew it is never going to be the same. Your behaviors have destroyed the trust and safety you once shared. You and your partner are going to have to rebuild a new relationship going forward. Many betrayed partners feel a lot of grief over the loss of the relationship they once had, in particular the loss of trust and safety. As such, your partner may be brokenhearted over promises you broke and commitments that were not kept. Validate that your partner has every right to feel these feelings and to doubt your honesty and commitment.

Topic 8: Apology and Amends

This part of your letter is your opportunity to express remorse and apologize for your betrayal. Your betrayed partner needs to hear that you feel regret, sadness, guilt, and shame about your behavior, and that you sincerely apologize and want to make amends.

Please understand that making amends is not the same as an apology; making amends is a commitment to make things right and to behave differently in the future. So, what are your commitments going forward? Do you agree to accept your partner's boundaries and provide your partner with the support that he or she needs? Share with your partner a brief outline of your recovery plan to demonstrate what your goals are and how you are going to live your life differently. Share what values you plan to adhere to and how this will affect your thoughts and behaviors.

Sample Emotional Restitution Letter

Dear Emma:

I am writing this letter to be accountable and to own all of the ways in which I have betrayed and harmed both you and our relationship. I want to show you that I truly understand the ways in which you were injured, and I want to let you know how I plan to help you heal and how I plan to re-earn your trust. Finally, I want to pledge my commitment to my recovery, to you, and to our marriage. I love you with all my heart, and I plan on spending the rest of my life earning your trust and co-creating our dream marriage and life together. I hope you can hear that these words are coming from my heart and soul.

I fully disclosed to you the extent of my addiction and betrayal during formal disclosure. I want to confirm now that the information I provided was accurate and complete. And I want to once again acknowledge that I repeatedly lied to you, kept important secrets from you, tried to manipulate you, and even blamed you for my actions. You were not at fault. My decisions were my own, and now that I am starting to understand how much damage and pain I was causing, I wish I had never done any of those things. I am responsible for all of that, and I am actively working to change my thinking and behavior so I don't do that to you ever again.

I know that my behavior led you to question our entire relationship, to wonder if I ever loved you at all. I also know that my betrayal has caused you to wonder if, when we were romantic and physically intimate, I was really 'there with you' or if I was thinking about some other woman. I understand this, and that you now question everything about my love and our relationship. This is my fault. I caused this confusion and doubt with my addiction and deception. I know that I would feel the same if you had done to me what I did to you. I also understand that you feel less present with the kids, that you worry they are internalizing blame for the tension in our marriage and home. Again, this is entirely my fault. As are the financial losses and expenses we've experienced and continue to experience as the result of my addiction. I feel terrible watching the stress and anxiety that all of this has caused you, especially knowing it is the direct result of my betrayal.

On numerous occasions, you questioned me about what I was doing. You made it clear that any type of sexual or romantic behavior outside our marriage was unacceptable and a violation of our marriage vows. You let me know that what I was doing, even though I wasn't willing to admit to my behaviors unless you caught me red-handed, was hurting our relationship and against your values, but I ignored that and continued to act out in my addiction.

To cover up my actions, I told you that you were just making things up in your mind because you're paranoid. I minimized your fears, ignored your opinions, disregarded your questions, and stomped on your feelings. I stonewalled you when you sought the truth. I caused you to question your reality. I tried to make you think the problems we were having were your fault. I acted as if I was the victim, rather than you. I disrespected your intelligence and your intuition. I continued to engage in these behaviors, even in the face of clear evidence to the contrary.

You have asked me many times why I did these things. That is something I have wondered as well. As part of treatment and therapy, I put together a lifelong timeline of my sexual behavior, and that has helped me understand when my addiction started and a bit about how that happened. My hope is that sharing this information with you will provide some explanation about my behavior. This is not, however, an excuse. This does not justify my choices. There is no excuse for the betrayal I perpetrated on you and our relationship.

I first learned to self-soothe with pornography and masturbation when I was 10. I used these behaviors as a way to avoid the chaos in my home when I was growing up. When my parents were drinking or fighting, I would go into my room and shut the door and escape into images and videos and masturbation. This behavior continued until we were married. While married, after my father's death, I couldn't deal with the grief and depression, so I self-medicated by using porn again, and in other ways. Then our son developed behavioral problems, which was overwhelming, and again, rather than facing my emotions, I acted out with porn and in other ways. I did not know how to handle these life stressors in a healthy, rational way because I never learned how to do that in childhood.

I hope you can see that even though my sex addiction hurt you deeply, you were not in any way the cause of it. It started long before I met you. I at times blamed you for my behaviors, but you were not ever at fault. Your reactions to my betrayal are completely justified. The trauma of my betrayal has put you on an emotional rollercoaster and made it difficult for you to trust me or anyone else. That is on me. And the fact that prior to formal disclosure I continued to withhold and keep secrets only made this worse for you. I want you to know that I understand that and feel awful about it.

I know that my behavior has deeply impacted your sense of self and your ability to trust and enjoy sex. I also understand that you feel shame about what has happened in our marriage, even though none of this is your fault. You worry about what our family and friends will think, and whether they will judge you for staying with me or somehow causing me to stray. I also worry about judgment from friends and family and how that might affect our lives. And, again, this is entirely my fault rather than yours. I have violated our relationship vows and ruined your ability to trust me and feel safe with me. I have caused you to wonder if you will ever be able to believe in me again, and I feel terrible that I've put you in this position.

From your impact letter and also from just spending time with you, I see how much my lying, secrets, and deceit hurt you. Thank you for sharing your vulnerability with me in your letter and in our life. It has helped me to really hear and feel the pain I've caused you. I will read and re-read your impact letter many more times, I am sure, as I continue my recovery, and I will continue to work on developing and feeling empathy. For now, I believe I have at least the beginnings of an awareness and appreciation for what you've experienced and continue to experience.

I want to validate that your experience is legitimate. Any person who was betrayed as I betrayed you would feel the same. I know that I would if I experienced this level of betrayal and deception. Your reactions to this were and continue to be completely and utterly normal, even though I have not always been supportive of that fact. I apologize for being angry when you were on an emotional rollercoaster. I blamed and criticized you for that, even though it was my fault, not yours. I was still making our life all about me.

I am ashamed of these actions, as well as the actions I took while active in my addiction. I feel sad when I think about what I have done to you, our relationship, and our family. I am truly sorry for my behavior and the pain and distress I've caused. I pledge to behave differently in the future, one day at a time.

I appreciate that you have been willing to stay with me despite the pain and suffering I've caused. I appreciate that you are giving me the chance to rebuild trust and intimacy in our relationship. I appreciate and respect the fact that you need to set certain boundaries to facilitate healing, trust, and intimacy. I am committed *to the second chance you are giving me. I am committed to my own recovery. I am committed to being the man I promised I would be when we got married. I am committed to giving you as much time and space as you need to heal, and to doing whatever I can to help.*

I want you to know that I am taking my addiction, my sobriety, and my process of recovery and healing seriously. I need this for myself as much as for you and our relationship and family. I do not like the man I became in my addiction, and I do not want to be that person any longer. My hope is to become my true self, which is the man I promised to be when we got married. This will not happen overnight. I will need to continually work on honesty and empathy, as well as on resolving my childhood trauma so it no longer drives my behaviors. My hope is that I will do these things a little bit better each day until I can finally look at myself in the mirror and be happy with the man looking back. I will be vigilant in my life and consistent in my recovery to achieve this.

I am incredibly grateful that you have expressed a willingness to walk beside me while I do this work.

Love,
Michael

Once you have completed the writing of your Emotional Restitution Letter, you will share this with your betrayed partner, preferably in the presence of your individual therapists and/or your couples therapist. This is the last step in the disclosure process and is a good way to create some closure around it.

Amends

As stated earlier, it is important that participating partners understand that making amends is not the same as giving an apology. Making amends means repairing the damage you've done through effort and action. An apology may be part of this, but it's only a small part.

Participating partners should also understand that making amends for relationship betrayal is not a single event. It is a process that takes time. Often you do it without meaning to, simply by expressing remorse for what you've done and consistently engaging in reliable and trustworthy behaviors. If you do not stay in a place of integrity during your healing process, though, the process can be derailed. Consider the case of Avery and Isla.

Case Example: Avery and Isla

After discovery of Avery's sexual addiction, Avery and Isla seemingly did everything right. They entered therapy both individually and as a couple. As much as Isla wanted to know everything about Avery's behaviors, they were wisely counseled in both individual and couple's therapy to wait for formal disclosure, which took place at the four-month mark of Avery's recovery.

Disclosure was well-monitored and well-supported, and Avery took and passed a polygraph so Isla could feel safe in her knowledge of the complete truth. Isla then wrote an impact letter and shared it in therapy with Avery. Avery said he felt terrible for what he'd done to his wife of 22 years, and he wrote and shared with her an emotional restitution letter similar to the sample letter shown above.

Unfortunately, Avery did not seem to 'get it' that saying he was going to make amends by making things right and *behaving differently in the future* meant that he actually had to do those things. Within a few months, he was skipping therapy sessions and 12-step meetings, and he'd stopped working the 12 steps with his sponsor. As he did so, he once again began to keep secrets and tell lies – not about his sexual life, but about other aspects of life.

At his six-month follow-up polygraph test, Avery passed a question about sexually acting out, but failed the question about keeping lies and telling secrets. Isla says she feels like their process of rebuilding trust and healing the relationship is back at zero, or maybe even somewhere even worse than zero. She says that even though Avery is not cheating or actively engaging in his sexual addiction, the lies and secrets hurt just as much. Isla says she feels like they need to revisit disclosure and start the process over, but Avery disagrees. Right now, they're at a standoff, and neither is hopeful about the future of their relationship.

As you can see from this case, honest, trustworthy, reliable behavior is critical during the healing process. Betrayed partners can often sense when there is ongoing acting out. Being one hundred percent invested in your recovery process is critical.

As you make amends for your betrayal, do not allow shame or pride to cloud your judgment. You must stop blaming others for your actions, and you must live differently going forward, placing your relationship ahead of your personal in-the-moment desires. You must also do the work of recovery and healing, coming to understand and accept your human failings, and admitting and taking responsibility for those failings in an open, non-defensive, and vulnerable way.

Participating partners, what you're being asked to do is no small task. Sincere expression of humility and remorse takes courage. But rest assured, this behavior will nearly always (though not always immediately) be noticed and appreciated by your betrayed partner, as long as your efforts are genuine.

Betrayed partners, what you're being asked to do is no small task either. If you receive an amends that you feel is genuine, and you start to see reliable trustworthy behavior, consider opening your heart in ways that will allow your participating partner back into the relationship. Forgiving doesn't mean forgetting; however, letting go of resentment is as healing for you as it is for your partner. Sometimes it is scary to open your heart and reinvest, but without taking that step, you'll never know if you can rebuild intimacy, trust, and deep emotional connection. So, look into your partner's eyes and give love a chance. Allow a space for love to grow.

CHAPTER FIVE:

Trauma, Accountability, and Empathy

Lingering Trauma

During the healing process, it's common for the betrayed partner's trauma (PTSD) symptoms to temporarily increase rather than decrease. They feel sadder, angrier, and more fearful about the participating partner's behavior and their relationship. They may be triggered to feel powerful emotions by even the smallest reminders of what happened.

One of the biggest mistakes that couples at this stage of healing can make is failing to communicate effectively about the betrayed partner's trauma symptoms. As a result, the participating partner feels like the betrayed partner is consistently overreacting, and the betrayed partner just feels crazy. And until the betrayed partner's trauma symptoms are identified and talked about, this unpleasant dynamic will continue.

For betrayed partners, the primary challenge here is to actively and intentionally bring pain, fear, and triggers back into your relationship. When you feel distressed or upset, you must go to your partner and share what you are feeling.

For participating partners, the challenge is listening to your betrayed partner's feelings and responding with empathy rather than judgment. Every time your partner brings you his or her fear, pain, or anger, you have an opportunity to help both your partner and your relationship heal. But only if you respond in a manner that shows your commitment to making amends, living differently, and saving your relationship.

The way you respond to your betrayed partner's trauma-driven thoughts and feelings is directly linked to your chances of staying together and healing your relationship.

Ineffective strategies include:

- **Minimizing:** It was just sex. There was no feeling or connection. It didn't mean anything to me. It barely qualifies as cheating.
- **Shifting Blame:** If I got more sex from you at home, I wouldn't have to sleep around to get my needs met.
- **Gaslighting:** If you think I'm checking out that woman, you're being paranoid.
- **Empty Promises:** I'm sorry about what I did. It was a mistake and it will never happen again. (And then doing nothing to change your behavior).
- **Withdrawal:** I can't stand all this fighting. I'll be in my office watching TV. Please let me be.
- **Pathologizing Your Partner's Responses:** You're trying to control every little thing that I do. That's what they call codependent. You need to go to therapy for that. It's really unhealthy and it's ruining our relationship.
- **Lying:** I'm telling you that I wasn't at a strip club. I had to work late. I don't know why you never believe me.
- **Avoiding:** I'm tired. It's been a long week at work and you're really suspicious and crazy. I don't have the energy for it. Let's talk about this some other time.
- **Arguing:** Why do I stay with you? You make every aspect of my life miserable. I'm not saying I'm cheating, but who could blame me if I was?

Clearly, these reactions are only going to cause more damage to your relationship. Part of healing your relationship post-disclosure is learning to respond to your partner with empathy and sensitivity. Betrayed partners experience events that trigger memories of the acting out behavior, and they need reassurance and compassionate understanding of their fears, thoughts and feelings.

Consider the case of Anne and Dave. Anne learned about Dave's one-night stands and porn use by finding information on his phone. Dave denied that he was cheating and said that Anne was misreading his phone. Then he told her she had no right to be looking at his phone, he deserved some privacy, and he was going to change all of his passwords and not share them with her. He also said that if she hadn't 'let herself go' and if he got more sex at home, he wouldn't need to think about other women, so, if he had cheated, though he still insisted he hadn't, it was all her fault, not his.

In the weeks that followed, Dave became more and more secretive. He was unwilling to discuss what happened. He continually insisted that he wasn't up to anything and Anne was being paranoid. She struggled to trust anything he said or did, even when she was right next to him and therefore knew the truth. As the days passed, they engaged in many painful battles—Dave telling lies and keeping secrets, Anne digging for truth. Eventually, the strain on their relationship proved too much and Anne filed for divorce.

There are many alternatives to these dysfunctional strategies that can calm and reassure your betrayed partner. Not only that, but many of these strategies can be the beginning of developing connection and intimacy in your relationship. Effective strategies include:

- **Empathy:** I can tell that you are feeling sad, and I know that I'm the cause of that. My heart hurts when I see you this way.
- **Accountability and Genuine Remorse:** Yes, I engaged in X, Y, and Z behaviors, and I tried to keep that secret. I even told you lies to cover up my behavior. I am truly sorry that I did that.
- **Reassurance:** I want to work to heal our relationship, and I am actively taking steps to do that, one of which is changing my behavior, another which is being open and honest with you at all times.
- **Open, Honest, Direct Communication:** I promise that from now on I will not keep secrets from you about anything, even little things, and I will not lie to you about anything, even little things. If I do keep a secret or tell you a lie, I promise to come clean within 24 hours.
- **Actions Matching Words:** I will take my recovery seriously. I will attend a 12-step meeting on Tuesday, Thursday, and Saturday night. I will engage in my own therapy and couples therapy with you weekly. I will keep you updated on my progress in treatment.
- **Reliable Behavior Over Time:** I will keep you informed of my whereabouts at all times. If I am running late, I will call or text to let you know where I am.

- **Transparency:** I will live my life with you as an open book. Rather than waiting for you to ask questions, I will volunteer any and all information that you might want to know.
- **Patience:** I understand that you are upset and angry with me, and I accept that it's my fault. I will give you as much time and space as you need to heal from my betrayal. When you are angry, I will let you be angry rather than trying to defend my actions.
- **Emotional Vulnerability:** I am afraid that you will leave me because of what I've done. I do not want to lose you or the life we have built together. I would feel very empty without you in my life.
- **Responding Sensitively:** I'm sorry that X happened and that it reminded you of my betrayal. I accept that you are feeling strong emotions right now, and that even though I haven't done anything wrong in the moment, it feels to you as if I did. If there is anything that I can do to help you in this moment, please let me know.
- **Following Treatment Recommendations:** My therapist has recommended weekly group therapy and multiple 12-step meetings each week. My schedule for group therapy is X, and my schedule for 12-step meetings is Y. If there is ever a reason for me to miss one of these sessions, I will let you know, and I will go to another session as a replacement.
- **Understanding:** I know that my past behavior is the cause of the pain you are feeling right now. I am sorry for that and I feel terrible that you're hurting. I am here for you if you want to talk to me. If you would rather not talk to me right now, I understand that and will respect it.
- **Gratitude:** I am grateful that when you found out about my betrayal you did not throw me out or pack your things and leave. That gives me hope that if I do the things I need to do for my recovery, our relationship can heal.
- **Appreciation:** I appreciate that you've chosen to stay together and to continue your role in our relationship and home life while I work on improving myself and my behaviors. Your willingness and patience mean a lot to me. I appreciate that while I'm struggling to be a better person, you have picked up the slack in our finances and obligations.
- **Listening:** I have heard what you said and would like to repeat back to you what I heard to make sure I fully understand. What I heard was X. Is that correct?
- **Giving Space:** I understand that you do not want to be sexual with me for a while, and that, at times, you may not want to be around me at all.

I accept that this is a result of my betrayal, and I will give you as much space as you need, as long as you understand that I do want to spend quality time with you.

- **Trying Not to be Reactive:** You are angry and you have every right to be angry. What I did was unforgivable. I accept your anger and my role in it. I would like to discuss the situation, so maybe we can find a way to move forward and heal.

- **Openness About Recovery:** I am currently working step 3 in my 12-step program. I am struggling with it because it requires me to turn my will and life over to a Higher Power. I am unable to do that with the punishing God that I was raised to believe in, so I'm having to adjust and seek some other form of spiritual connection. Something more loving and supportive.

- **Genuineness:** I had an okay day today. Some things went right. A few of them were X and Y. A few things did not go the way I'd hoped they might. In particular, I feel disappointed and angry about Z. In the past, this is the sort of disappointment I might have acted out over. Now, in recovery, I am sharing about it with you, and I will also speak with my sponsor.

Consider the case of Sarah and Ira. Sarah learned about Ira's sexual affair by finding information on his phone. Ira took accountability and ownership of his betrayal, entered therapy, and followed his therapist's recommendations. He was completely open and honest with Sarah about his actions, and during their healing process he was consistently honest and reliable.

One morning, Sarah expressed concerns about a few longer periods of unaccounted-for time because, in the past, when Ira would disappear for a while, he was usually acting out. As a result of Sarah's expressed concern, Ira agreed to keep her in the loop on his whereabouts at all times, and he installed tracking software on his phone to help with that.

Another morning, Sarah was feeling insecure about the relationship and was starting to worry that Ira was again cheating. As a result, she looked at Ira's phone. She did not find anything on his phone that was a concern. When Ira came into the room, Sarah owned up to the fact that she was looking at his phone, saying she needed to do that to feel safe. Ira's response was, "That's OK. You have full access to everything. You don't need to ask for permission, and you don't need to feel bad or apologize."

Sarah couldn't help but notice the huge difference in Ira's responses to her. In the past, he would have lied about where he was during his unaccounted-for time, and he would have been angry that she was looking at his phone. Ira's new attitude toward her trauma was incredibly reassuring for her. These and similar events created a positive shift in the relationship for Sarah, and a compelling step forward for Ira.

Accountability

Accountability involves not only taking ownership and responsibility for the betrayal, but for rectifying the situation and making things right. Betrayed partners need to see the participating partner taking full ownership with a genuine attitude of guilt and remorse. If betrayed partners don't see genuine guilt and remorse, it's difficult for them to reopen their hearts and risk being hurt again.

Accountability is the key to unlocking the possibility of forgiveness and relationship healing. If participating partners don't become accountable, both partners will stay stuck. The relationship becomes a frozen wasteland of resentment.

If you're the participating partner, you may be thinking to yourself, "Why is this all my fault? My betrayed partner also has a role in our relationship dysfunction." That may well be true, but, as stated repeatedly throughout this book, healing the offense of the betrayal supersedes whatever infraction(s) your betrayed partner may have committed. Healing from the betrayal that you committed has to come first.

There are numerous ways for participating partners to develop accountability in their personal recovery and within the relationship. A few of the more common methods include:

- Get a 12-step sponsor and check in with that person on a regular basis.
- Check in with group therapy and support group members on a regular basis.
- Install filtering/monitoring/tracking software on all digital devices.
- Turn the family finances over to the betrayed partner (or at least give the betrayed partner full access).

- Amend any lies or disclose any secrets (about anything) within 24 hours.
- Be rigorously honest in the relationship and all other aspects of life.
- Be where you say you will be when you say you will be there.
- Check in with your betrayed partner daily to make sure he or she knows everything that's going on in your life.

Consistently engaging in these accountability focused behaviors is a great way for participating partners to restore relationship trust, and to slowly but steadily lessen the impact of their betrayed partner's trauma symptoms. These actions will also help participating partners stay on track with their process of recovery and behavior change.

Empathy: The SUPPORT Model

At this point in the healing process, it is vital that participating partners begin to display empathy for their betrayed partner. Empathy is the ability to feel and share in someone else's pain as though you were feeling it yourself. This means that when your betrayed partner brings his or her pain to you, instead of trying to deflect, minimize, or talk your partner out of it, you should enter into and share the pain.

To do this, try to understand exactly what your partner is experiencing. This means actively listening and asking questions about your partner's thoughts and feelings. You must also let go of all thoughts about what you're going to say next and how you're going to try to fix things and make things better.

Of course, for participating partners, empathy is not easy. After all, they've been avoiding it throughout the cheating because who wants to think about the feelings of the person you're betraying in the middle of the betrayal? Participating partners have either shut that part of themselves down, or they're extremely out of practice with it.

It's common for betrayed partners to get triggered and experience fear and anxiety related to the betrayal. For example, the betrayed partner might see something that reminds them of the betrayal. Recognizing this, the following SUPPORT model is designed to help participating partners respond with empathy to their betrayed partner's emotions and experience.

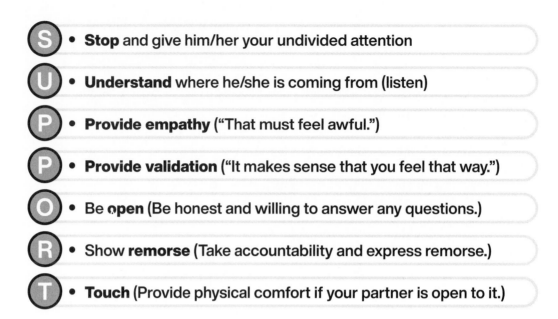

- **S** • **Stop** and give him/her your undivided attention
- **U** • **Understand** where he/she is coming from (listen)
- **P** • **Provide empathy** ("That must feel awful.")
- **P** • **Provide validation** ("It makes sense that you feel that way.")
- **O** • Be **open** (Be honest and willing to answer any questions.)
- **R** • Show **remorse** (Take accountability and express remorse.)
- **T** • **Touch** (Provide physical comfort if your partner is open to it.)

When your betrayed partner is triggered, the first step is to simply STOP and give your partner your undivided attention. This action helps both you and your partner feel that his or her concern is of the utmost importance. Do not minimize, deflect, or rush forward to fix things or to take care of your own business.

The second step in the model is to UNDERSTAND what is going on with your betrayed partner by really listening. This means trying to understand every aspect of what has upset your partner, including everything that led up to the event, what he or she thinks about it now, and what he or she is feeling.

The first two steps of the model should take some time, especially if you're effectively and actively listening. As part of this process, you may want to ask questions and reflect back what you've heard, making sure you've understood your betrayed partner. As you do this, be aware that your first instinct may be to rationalize, deny, and shift responsibility. Do not succumb to that instinct. Giving in to that is counterproductive at best.

If you can do the first two steps of SUPPORT properly, the outcome of your conversation is likely to move into a more positive realm—a place where empathy and validation will have meaning and constructive impact.

The third step is to PROVIDE EMPATHY. Examples of empathic statements are as follows:

- I sense that you're hurting, and that makes me hurt with you.
- If you had done to me what I did to you, I would feel exactly what you're feeling.
- I've dragged you through the wringer, and I understand that your confusion and anger are my fault.

The fourth step is to PROVIDE VALIDATION for what your partner is thinking and feeling. Examples of validating statements are as follows:

- You have every right to feel the way you are feeling.
- When I do X, it's only logical that you worry I might be cheating again.
- The suspicions you had about my cheating were correct, even though I lied and said they weren't. So I totally understand why you're struggling to trust me now.

The fifth step is to be OPEN to any response or questions your betrayed partner has about your empathetic and validating statements. Do not judge your partner's reactions or try to defend yourself or your statements. Answer all questions as honestly as you possibly can.

The sixth step is to show REMORSE by taking accountability for what you've done. As part of this, your betrayed partner may need reassurance that you're committed to the relationship, and you're now being 100 percent faithful. Your partner may inquire about your whereabouts and expenditures. Your partner may need to hear your statements several times to process and understand. If so, be patient, remain open, and continue to provide reassurance.

The final step is to provide comfort via TOUCH if your betrayed partner seems open to that. A hug when your partner is feeling pain can go a long way. If, however, your partner does not seem open to physical touch, you'll need to respect that boundary.

Throughout the SUPPORT process, it is critical that participating partners demonstrate an attitude of accountability and remorse (step 6). Statements such as, "It breaks my heart that my behavior has caused you so much pain," and, "I regret that my behavior has hurt you so badly," are always helpful. Even though it may seem counterintuitive to keep apologizing all the time, your partner may need to hear how sorry you are over and over.

> **Note:** The SUPPORT model requires both parties to participate. Betrayed partners, you must bring your pain and concerns to the participating partner so those issues can be discussed and addressed.

Case Study: Devin and LaTonya

Devin is a 32-year-old recovering sex and porn addict, married to 25-year-old LaTonya for three years. Six months ago, LaTonya found out about Devin's secret sex life because he was fired from his job for viewing porn and using hookup apps both at work and away from work on company-owned devices. Before getting fired, Devin had received a verbal warning about his behavior, and then a written warning that clearly stated he would be fired if he continued to act out in this way.

When he lost his job, Devin came clean about his addiction with LaTonya, and she agreed to stay with him if he entered therapy and a process of recovery, which he has done. He has not had any slips or relapses since that time, but until he and LaTonya went through the process of therapeutic disclosure, he kept a number of secrets about what he had done, with whom, and what those behaviors had cost him, (this was not the first time he'd been fired for sexual misbehavior).

Both Devin and LaTonya are relieved that everything is now out in the open, and that Devin is getting the professional and 12-step help that he's needed for more than a decade. LaTonya is also glad to know that her suspicions about Devin's behavior, which he once vehemently denied, were actually on target. For most of their relationship, she'd suspected that Devin might be cheating, but his denials were so earnest and consistent that eventually she began to wonder if the issue was with her, not Devin.

LaTonya is seeing a therapist individually, as well as a couples therapist with Devin. At first, she resisted the idea of getting help for herself, but now that she finally has a calm voice of reason in her life (her therapist), she can't imagine why she didn't seek help sooner. At this point, much of what LaTonya is working on involves her continued, often unwarranted, emotional reactivity with Devin. She knows that Devin is actively working his program of recovery. She knows everything that happened in his addiction, and that he's trying his best to be rigorously honest and restore relationship trust. But there are times when she's just not on board with all of that, and the trauma of betrayal surfaces.

One recent example involved Devin's new job. He states that he's thrilled to have found work that he likes and fits his skill set. He's also happy to bring in a significant paycheck to help support the household. For LaTonya, however, the new job has created nothing but fear and anger, mostly because Devin now has a new set of employer-supplied digital devices, and she's afraid he'll use them to act out. She talked about this with her individual therapist and was encouraged to share her feelings with Devin.

When LaTonya told Devin about her fears, Devin admits that he was initially angry that LaTonya was struggling to feel happiness about his exciting new job. For him, the job was a sign that recovery was working and working well in his life, and it hurt that she viewed it differently. He did not, however, express his disappointment with LaTonya's feelings. Instead, he implemented the support model that he and LaTonya have been utilizing in their couples counseling sessions.

Instead of expressing anger and disappointment that LaTonya was not happy for him, he stopped and listened to what she had to say. When he did that, he quickly and easily understood that the issue was not that he got a great new job, it's that he suddenly had a new smartphone and laptop and, if he so chose, he could use those devices to act out as he'd done in the past.

Once Devin understood what was triggering LaTonya's trauma, he was able to provide empathy and validation for her feelings. To this end, he told her, "I am so sorry you're having these feelings, and I completely understand why you're having them. If you had secretly used digital devices at work to cheat on me, and now you had a new job with new digital devices, I'd be feeling the same fear that you're having. I want you to know that you have every right to feel this way. It's only natural that you'd worry I might relapse."

Once the nature of the issue was out in the open, and Devin had validated and displayed empathy for LaTonya's feelings, they were able to have a productive conversation about how Devin could put safeguards in place to stop himself from misusing company equipment and relapsing in his addiction. For starters, Devin suggested that they install the same filtering/monitoring/tracking software on his work-owned digital devices as they'd put on his personal digital devices. With this, LaTonya immediately felt much of her fear and anger go away.

As they worked through the issue of Devin's new job and digital devices, he repeatedly said, "It breaks my heart that my behaviors have caused you to feel this way. I feel horrible about the trauma that I've caused, and I am deeply and truly sorry about the damage I perpetrated on our relationship. Please know that I'm doing everything I can to heal from my addiction and to re-earn your trust." At the end of the conversation, after the protective software had been installed, Devin asked if he could hug LaTonya to support her and show his love for her. She thought about it for a moment and then agreed.

Devin and LaTonya discussed this incident and its resolution in their next couples counseling session, with both of them feeling as if they'd taken a significant step forward in their process of healing. For Devin, his commitment to recovery and to rebuilding his relationship was affirmed in a powerful way. For LaTonya, her ability to trust and believe in Devin's recovery and ongoing honesty were greatly strengthened.

This breakthrough does not mean that LaTonya will never again experience emotional reactivity related to her relationship trauma. Nor does it mean that Devin will willingly and effectively implement the SUPPORT model every time LaTonya is triggered. Most likely, progress for both partners will be two steps forward, one step back. Over time, however, the SUPPORT model, if they continue to utilize it both in and out of therapy, will help them to better understand and empathize with one another, to rebuild relationship trust, and to create a new sense of relational connection and intimacy.

CHAPTER SIX:

Rebuilding Trust and Intimacy

Putting Your Relationship First

During this next phase of healing, you will need to place your relationship at the top of your priority list, and to make ten commitments toward rebuilding trust and intimacy. If you notice that your partner is forgetting or not honoring one of these commitments, you can provide a gentle reminder. If your partner reminds you about one of these commitments, you can step back, take a deep breath, and remember that right now your relationship is your top priority. Then you can redirect yourself back to your commitments.

As you might suspect, making your relationship your number one priority is easier said than done. If you're like most couples, there is a lot going on in your life. One or both of you likely has a job. There is a home to maintain. You may have children or pets. You'll have siblings, in-laws, friends, neighbors, and all sorts of other people demanding your time and focus. All of those things are important. Very important.

But are they as important as saving your relationship?

- **Job:** If putting your relationship ahead of your job costs you your job, you have to wonder if that's the sort of job you really want to have. Do you live to work, or work to live? Putting your relationship first means your life is bigger and more important than your job. Can you make that commitment? If you're struggling with this, ask yourself which you would grieve more if it ended: your job or your relationship. Then ask yourself which would be harder to replace.

- **Home:** Is a home really a home if your significant other is not part of it? Probably not. So if it's a choice between couples therapy and mowing the lawn, again, put your relationship first.

- **Children and Pets:** Your children and your pets are integral to your relationship. More so than anything else. That said, part of taking care of them is taking care of your intimate connection with your partner. Imagine how your children and pets would suffer if your relationship were to end. If you have to miss a soccer game or the dog doesn't get as long a walk as he wants because you need to devote some extra time to relationship healing, so be it. A short-term disappointment for your child or pet is ultimately going to be far less painful than a divorce.

- **Family and Friends:** If your family and friends truly love you and care about you, they will understand your need to focus on healing your relationship with your spouse. In fact, they will support you in this endeavor. They will be happy that you're having date night and therefore can't spend the evening with them.

Yes, putting your relationship above all else requires you to make sacrifices in other areas of life. But if you don't put your relationship first, you'll end up making bigger sacrifices. Without your relationship, you will lose much of what you value. When you recognize this fact, it's a lot easier to accept the minor setbacks and inconveniences that focusing on your relationship creates in other areas of life.

It is suggested that when the two of you make the conscious decision to put your relationship first, you sit down facing each other, look each other in the eyes, and speak this commitment aloud. Then you can discuss the areas of your life that may be affected by this choice, and you can agree that, despite these potential issues, you are both fully invested in the process of healing your relationship and doing so is your top priority.

Once this decision is made, you should agree to the ten commitments outlined later in this chapter.

Case Study: Juan Carlos and Erica

Juan Carlos and Erica have been married ten years and have two sons, ages 8 and 5. Six months ago, Juan Carlos found hookup apps on Erica's phone and realized she'd been cheating on him. After several weeks of staggered discovery and threats by Juan Carlos to take the boys and leave the relationship, Erica agreed to see a therapist. After assessment, the therapist concluded that Erica, who'd been having multiple affairs, one night stands, sexting, and using porn compulsively, was sexually addicted. Erica was then referred to a Certified Sex Addiction Therapist and her recovery began in earnest.

Eventually, at the urging of his best friend, Juan Carlos also entered a process of healing, with an individual therapist and a weekly support group for betrayed spouses. Since that time, Erica has provided therapeutic disclosure, complete with a polygraph test, which allowed Juan Carlos to finally take some major steps forward in his process of healing.

For her part, Erica has been diligent about therapy and recovery. She has also worked very hard to become honest with Juan Carlos about all aspects of her life. She has filtering and monitoring software on her phone and tablet, and Juan Carlos receives regular reports that tell him when she's online and what she does online. She has not cheated on him in any way since initial discovery, though she did keep a number of secrets prior to the therapeutic disclosure.

After therapeutic disclosure, Juan Carlos and Erica were both relieved that everything was finally out in the open, but they were unsure about what to do next. Both wanted to know, "How do we start putting our relationship back together? We're tired of living in this state of constant anxiety and distress, but we don't know how to move forward."

Ten Commitments

The uncertainty faced by Juan Carlos and Erica is a natural place to find yourself after disclosure. You can't help but wonder, *What's next? When can we start living a normal life where we're not constantly on edge? And what do we do to get to that place?* Answering these questions is what the remainder of this book is about.

Before proceeding, however, it is important to know that during this phase there will be times when the pain of the original betrayal will resurface. When that happens, participating partners must continue to respond with empathy, compassion, openness, and sensitivity, remembering to use the SUPPORT model. At the same time, betrayed partners need to remember that the betrayal is not happening all over again in the moment. It may feel that way, but that's not reality. They are simply having a post-traumatic reaction that is perfectly normal and will pass.

Now it is time for you and your partner to make the following ten commitments.

Commitment #1: Focus on Forgiveness

During this phase of healing, both of you need to keep an open mind about forgiveness and be patient regarding forgiveness. Forgiveness is a long-term proposition, not something that happens immediately.

Before forgiveness can occur, betrayed partners must believe that healing and moving on are possible. This does not mean they must forget what happened. It means they must believe that it's possible to release their resentments about what happened. It means they must believe that people make mistakes, people learn from mistakes, and people grow and change based on their mistakes.

At the same time, participating partners must take accountability for their transgressions and change their behavior moving forward. They must be open and accountable in all aspects of life. Most of all, they must be sensitive to their betrayed partner's experience of trauma by demonstrating remorse about the past while exhibiting behavior in the present that puts the relationship first.

These behaviors by both the betrayed and participating partner help feelings of anger and resentment dissipate. Not quickly, mind you, but eventually. You will both have to be patient. Betrayed partners must be willing to eventually forgive, and participating partners must be vigilant in their recovery work and their sensitivity to the betrayed partner's pain. They may need to repeatedly apologize and demonstrate remorse for many months before forgiveness starts to occur. And even then, progress will be slow and incremental.

For betrayed partners, actively working on feelings of anger and resentment is incredibly important. You should continue to examine these feelings in individual therapy, in couples counseling, and face-to-face with your partner when the two of you can do so in an evenhanded, productive fashion.

To this end, as a betrayed partner it is necessary that you bring your pain to your participating partner when it comes up so that it doesn't fester and grow. Holding onto your resentments is a recipe for health problems, depression, and anxiety. It is also a major roadblock to rebuilding trust and healing your intimate connection.

Participating partners, in addition to receiving forgiveness from their betrayed partner, might need to forgive themselves. In fact, they often find that forgiving themselves takes longer than earning forgiveness from their betrayed partner.

As a participating partner, you may be carrying guilt and shame about your behavior that borders on debilitating. This guilt and shame may cause you to feel as if you don't deserve love and forgiveness. If so, you need to keep in mind the fact that all humans make mistakes and have regrets. And making a mistake doesn't mean you are a mistake. It's okay to forgive yourself for what you did. Moreover, doing the right things to help your partner heal and to heal your relationship will help you heal, too. When things get difficult and you're beating yourself up, simply do the next right thing to keep moving forward. Doing this will help both you and your betrayed partner in the process of forgiveness.

Commitment #2: Rebuild Trust

The only way to rebuild the trust that has been destroyed by relationship betrayal is to demonstrate reliable behavior over time. Understanding this fact is especially important for participating partners. Because of your deception while cheating, your betrayed partner is now suspicious and anxious about your words, actions, and whereabouts. To remedy this, you need to speak the truth, you need to be where you say you will be, and you need to be there when you say you are going to be there. Your actions need to match your words exactly. There is no room for even minor falsehoods or white lies.

In his book *The Four Agreements*, Don Miguel Ruiz states that to develop integrity and trust, you must be "impeccable with your word."[1] Nowhere is this more applicable than with couples healing from infidelity. If you're running five minutes late, call your betrayed partner so he or she knows where you are and why you are running late. This will help to rebuild trust, and it will prevent your betrayed partner from making up stories about what you might be doing. If you forgot to take the trash out last night like your partner asked, admit it. Don't sneak out the back door in the morning, take it to the curb, and pretend you did it last night.

As the participating partner, you need to be honest in this way in *all* aspects of life. When your betrayed partner sees you being honest with everyone, all the time, no matter what, it's a lot easier to accept the idea that you're being honest with him or her, too.

Betrayed partners also have a role in rebuilding trust. First and foremost, you need to speak up about what you're thinking and feeling. If you worry about what your partner does on his or her lunch hour at work, ask for a mid-lunch phone call, possibly with a texted photo showing where your partner is and who your partner is with. You also need to be willing to accept the possibility that your partner, no matter how much he or she has lied in the past, is now telling the truth about all of his or her behavior, and that he or she is doing so without investigation or prompting by you.

Of course, as a betrayed partner, you are likely struggling to accept that your participating partner is actually doing what's necessary to rebuild trust. After all, your partner has kept so many secrets, told so many lies, and shifted blame for the infidelity onto others (including you) so many times that it's almost impossible to believe this change is occurring, even after therapeutic disclosure. As with forgiveness, you need to open your mind to the possibility that your partner is now being rigorously honest because he or she truly wants to re-earn your trust.

Commitment #3: Rebuild Your Friendship

Relationship expert John Gottman demonstrates in his research that it takes five positive interactions in your relationship to counterbalance one negative interaction.[2] This ratio of five positives for every one negative is the general rule of thumb for a relationship to remain satisfying and committed. Unfortunately, sexual betrayal is a huge negative and extremely destructive to your relationship. Most couples find that with sexual betrayal the 5:1 ratio is an underestimate, and many more than five positives are needed.

Whatever the ratio, your relationship needs the healing power provided by experiencing fun and enjoyment together. Most of what you've done so far in the process of healing has been either painful or hard work (or both). Now it is time to engage in some fun, enjoyable, non-stressful relationship-building activities. For many couples, this can look and feel a lot like dating.

Think back to the beginning of your relationship. What initially drew you to one another? What activities did you enjoy together? You should also look at things you've enjoyed after you settled down together. What mutual hobbies do you have? What activities do you both enjoy? In what ways have you enjoyed supporting your significant other? What have you talked about doing together but not gotten around to? Are there dreams the two of you have that were put on hold for some reason? If so, would it be possible to rekindle those dreams now?

In the space below, working together, create a list of things you've enjoyed together in the past and that you think you'll enjoy together again, along with things you'd like to do together in the future. There are no right or wrong answers with this exercise. Just make an exhaustive list of all the possible fun activities you can do or would like to do together.

Activities

....

....

....

....

....

....

....

....

....

....

....

....

....

....

After you've completed this list, identify and schedule at least one date night during your week. Your date night(s) should be the same night(s) every week if possible. Consider your date night(s) to be a standing appointment, and do not for any reason schedule anything else on a date night (remember your agreement to put your relationship first, no matter what). If an emergency or some event that is absolutely unavoidable gets in the way of a date night, reschedule that date for another night.

Keep in mind that date nights are not about working through your issues. Date nights are for fun. You don't need to re-create dates from your past, but you do need to act as if you're still in the dating process, where your time together is both fun and revealing of your and your partner's personalities. Please try very hard to keep date nights fun and lighthearted. This is not the time to revisit or attempt painful healing work. Keep your conversations focused on positive thoughts and feelings and what you're enjoying in the moment.

At the same time, you should stay attuned to your partner. What is your partner thinking? How is your partner feeling? Make it your goal to help your partner have as much fun as possible during date night. You don't need to put a lot of pressure on yourself to accomplish that goal; just keep it in the back of your mind as you interact with your significant other. Most of all, try to forget (temporarily, at least) about the betrayal, focusing instead on being friends and enjoying each other's company.

Our standing date night is : _____.

Commitment #4: Acts of Love and Kindness

Engaging in acts of love and kindness without expecting anything in return—being nice *just because*—is an important part of romantic relationships. And the door swings both ways on this one. Both participating partners and betrayed partners are hopefully, at this stage of healing, ready to perform *and receive* at least a few acts of love and kindness.

These acts can be obvious things like foot rubs, cards, flowers, candy, nice text messages, fixing something around the house without being asked, etc. It can also be less obvious things like acknowledging your partner's efforts toward healing, expressing gratitude to still be together, and buying (or making) a gift that will have special meaning to your partner—a gift based on something unique that only you know about your partner.

As you and your partner begin to reintroduce acts of love and kindness into your relationship, it may feel awkward. You may wonder, especially if you are the partic-ipating partner, how your gesture will be received. And that's okay. It might even be a little bit romantic. Think back to when you were dating and the first time you attempted an act of love and kindness to show your future partner how much you cared. What did that feel like? Most likely, it was exciting and scary at the same time. Why shouldn't it feel like that again?

If you're the betrayed partner, you may feel, as the participating partner attempts to reintroduce acts of love and kindness into your relationship, that he or she is attempting to manipulate you. If so, take a step back and remember your agree-ment to put your relationship first, and be willing to accept the idea that your partner may be doing this out of love rather than trying to control your feelings. Open your mind to trust and friendship, and do your best to accept the offering as a genuine act with no strings attached.

In the same vein, whether you are the participating partner or the betrayed partner, you must check your motives with every act of love and kindness you give. Make sure you are engaging in this act simply because you love your significant other and want to do something nice. If you have an ulterior motive (even something noble like wanting your partner to feel happy), you need to discard it. The only expectation you should attach to your offering is that you will feel good about giving it. Your partner's response is not yours to control, so don't try.

Commitment #5: Present a United Front

Couples who want to stay together make that fact known by working together on their issues and presenting a united front to their children, in-laws, other family members, and friends. When they talk to their children about what's going on, they first agree upon what will be said and who will say it, and then, together, they sit the children down and talk to them—sticking to the agreed-upon script. They always make it clear that despite what happened, they love each other and are committed to staying together and repairing the relationship.

Another way to present a united front is to ask friends and family who know about the betrayal to help you with your commitments to recovery, healing, and your relationship. Participating partners can ask their friends to help them with honesty, calling them out if/when they say something the other person doubts. Learning to be honest takes time, effort, and practice, and having a coach or two can be extremely helpful. Meanwhile, betrayed partners can ask friends, especially those who've survived infidelity, for emotional reality checks.

Juan Carlos, for example, after Erica worked to create and frame a painting of his kind heart and soul (an act of love and kindness), initially felt that Erica did this only to get back in his good graces. He shared this with his best friend and got an unexpected response. "Do you really think Erica would create something that beautiful just to manipulate you? Because I don't. Maybe she did it because she wants you to know how much she loves you." Then Juan Carlos and his friend walked through the effort Erica was consistently making to repair their relationship.

With that reality check, Juan Carlos was suddenly able to feel the love expressed in the painting. That evening, when Erica came home from work, she found Juan Carlos in front of the painting admiring it. "It's beautiful," he said. "Thank you."

Then they hugged—a genuine, meaningful, "I love you" hug. A few days later, their couples therapist asked what happened after the hug. They smiled and said that nothing happened; the hug was enough for both of them. Then Juan Carlos said, "It was the first time I've felt truly connected with Erica since discovery. I also finally felt like yes, we really are healing. It was real. It felt like maybe all the pain is going to be worth it."

Commitment #6: Effective Anger Management

Every couple has disagreements. And that's actually a good thing. When you disagree with your partner, you learn things about your partner and your partner learns things about you. And that knowledge can bring you closer together rather than pushing you apart, but only if you learn to communicate your disagreements productively and respectfully. Typically, this involves:

- Recognizing that you are allies, not foes. With this, you can fight *the problem* rather than each other. Winning doesn't mean getting your way. It means resolving the disagreement (even if you can only resolve it by simply agreeing to respect each other's opinion).
- Identifying the specific focus of the current disagreement and staying focused on that disagreement, rather than bringing up other issues and resentments.
- Placing a time limit on loaded discussions, such as 30 minutes. When the time is up, if the disagreement is not settled, you can agree to continue the discussion for another 30 minutes or to table it, perhaps waiting to discuss it further in couples therapy.
- Agreeing to not argue before work, before bed, in bed, in front of the children, in the car, while drinking, or in public spaces. Arguing at the wrong time of day (when you're stressed or tired, for example), in the wrong place, in the wrong frame of mind, or in front of others, tends to exacerbate rather than resolve conflicts.
- Agreeing to refrain from name-calling and other forms of emotional abuse.
- Agreeing to refrain from hitting, throwing things, slamming doors, and other forms of threats and violence.
- Agreeing to ask for help (most likely in the form of couples counseling) if you are truly stuck and unable to resolve your disagreement.

Commitment #7: Rebuild Emotional Intimacy

Good relationships are built on emotional intimacy, not sexual intimacy. In fact, good sex is also built on emotional intimacy. If you feel a deep connection with your partner, you will have a stronger relationship, a better sex life together, and a more enjoyable friendship. But after a betrayal, emotional intimacy can be strained and diminished. This loss is not repaired simply because the cheating stops and both partners enter a process of recovery.

To restore (or perhaps create for the first time) a sense of emotional intimacy in your relationship, it is suggested that you set some time aside each day, usually, though not necessarily, at the end of the day, for a mutual check-in. At this pre-arranged time, you and your partner should sit down in a quiet space where you will not be disturbed. You can then share your thoughts and feelings. Mark and Deborah Laaser created a couples check-in called the FANOS that has been very helpful for couples.[3] The FANOS is an anacronym couples can use to share what is going on with them on a daily basis.

FANOS

A daily check-in for couples from the Greek word 'phainos' which means "to bring to light"

by Mark Laaser, M.Div, PhD
& Debbie Laaser, MA, LMFT

Feelings – state your feelings (not your thoughts!).

Affirmation – give your spouse an affirmation or say "thank you" for something.

Needs – ask for something you need today, not necessarily from your spouse (be specific!).

Own – something you did or said that you take responsibility/apologize for.

Sobriety – report on the status of your sobriety.

From *Shattered Vows* pg 184–185 by Debbie Laaser, MA, LMFT
Copyright © Faithful & True 2007

Both partners should check in using this formula as a way of knowing what the other is thinking and feeling. Take turns going first, and recognize that this does not need to be a long, drawn-out discussion. It's simply a brief, yet honest, and vulnerable daily check-in that helps the two of you be honest, stay connected, and develop intimacy.

Commitment #8: Couples Therapy

Sometimes couples think that after disclosure, as long as the participating partner stays faithful and works his or her program of recovery, everything should be fine. But that's not how it works. Both partners are emotionally raw and vulnerable at this point, and little things (even if they are completely unrelated to the betrayal) can somehow become big things. When those little things become big things, they can drive a wedge between the partners that threatens their commitment to save the relationship.

Erica and Juan Carlos experienced this in multiple ways, and they found themselves arguing and shutting each other out even as they were both doing so many other things right in their process of healing. One of the biggest issues was that Erica felt Juan Carlos did not do his fair share of work around the house and caring for the children. In therapy, Juan Carlos stated that he did not think this was true, that he helped coach both sons' sports teams, kept the yard looking nice, and looked after the boys when Erica was at her therapy and her weekly support group.

Both Erica and Juan Carlos admitted in counseling that 'division of labor' had been an issue throughout their marriage, long before Erica's betrayal. Neither felt this was a deal-breaker in their relationship, but both felt it was an issue that was holding them back at times in their process of healing.

After some guided discussion in therapy, it turned out that neither of them minded the bulk of their chores. In fact, each of them enjoyed a lot of what they did around the house and with the children. There were a few tasks, however, that they both despised, and that was the real bone of contention. Eventually, they made a list of those tasks and divvied them up, agreeing to either alternate or share the chores they really hated. With one task, they agreed that rather than taking it on themselves, they would hire a professional.

After this work in therapy, they still had the occasional squabble over domestic tasks, but mostly they were each happy to perform the chores to which they'd committed.

Commitment #9: Shared Peacefulness or Spirituality

Depending on your individual belief systems and your belief system as a couple, it may be helpful to actively invite the sacred into your lives and to engage in this work together. If one or both of you are not spiritual or religious, this might include spending time in nature—hiking, enjoying the beach, boating, camping, gardening, or whatever else you can think of. Even something as simple as sitting in the backyard and roasting marshmallows over a fire can bring you a sense of serenity and connection with nature.

If you are a faith-based couple, praying together, studying scripture together, and attending church, synagogue or mosque together can help you feel more connected as a couple, more connected to your Higher Power, and more connected to your spiritual community.

If you're spiritual but not religious, you can meditate together, discuss what your spiritual connection looks and feels like, and create spiritual rituals that are meaningful to you either individually or together. You can also practice yoga, tai chi, and other forms of spiritual activity and connection. Even exercising together can be a form of mutual spiritual connection.

In the space below, each partner should identify three spiritual or religious things that he or she will do as an individual.

Betrayed partner

    1 _____

    2 _____

    3 _____

Participating partner

    1 _____

    2 _____

    3 _____

Now, together, identify three (or more) spiritual or religious things you will do together as a couple.

1 _____

2 _____

3 _____

Commitment #10: Patience

It is important to understand that your relationship will not repair itself overnight. You will not finish the process of therapeutic disclosure and suddenly enjoy every waking moment of your time with one another. Moving your relationship from a place of stress and pain to a place of trust and fun is not something that happens automatically or immediately. There is a lot of effort involved. There is a lot of time involved. And there is a lot of backsliding into stress and pain along the way.

You will need to be patient. If you are, and if each of you is doing the things that he or she needs to do to heal the betrayal, rebuild relationship trust, and renew your friendship with and enjoyment of one another, you will wake up one morning, look at your partner, and think, "Wow, this is great. I had no idea it could be this great. Even before the betrayal it wasn't this good. We weren't this connected. We weren't this in love. We weren't this happy."

But that's not likely to happen today or even tomorrow. For many couples, healing from betrayal can be a process that takes three, four, or even five years. The good news today is that when it does happen, all the pain you're dealing with today and all the hard work you're doing today will most definitely be worthwhile.

Giving and Receiving Gentle Reminders (When Necessary)

Putting your relationship first no matter what and following through on the ten commitments outlined in this chapter is not an easy process, and neither you nor your partner will do it perfectly. There will be days where you feel like you're moving backward instead of forward. There will be days when you just don't want to do the things you've committed to do. Your partner will, at times, experience the same feelings.

This is normal. Do not fret. But neither should you give in to those feelings. You and your partner must stay strong, remembering that the most important thing in your life is your relationship. This means that in your moments of weakness you must speak up and tell your partner what you're thinking and feeling (perhaps during your daily check-in). You must let your partner give you strength in those moments. When it's your partner who is feeling unmotivated, you need to return the favor, providing love, empathy, and encouragement.

If you are not 'feeling it' on a particular day and aren't honest about that fact, don't be surprised if your partner calls you out on this. Feel free to do the same when the situation is reversed, but be gentle. This is not a referendum on your character or inner resolve. It's simply a reminder of your mutual top priority—rebuilding your relationship—and the commitments you've made to make that happen.

Erica and Juan Carlos experienced this type of issue around Sunday morning church one week. Erica and the boys were dressed and ready to go, but Juan Carlos was wearing sweats and sitting on the couch watching TV. What Erica wanted to say was, "Hey, get dressed and get in the car so we're not late to church. You know how much I hate walking in late."

Erica knew, however, from her work in therapy and couples counseling, that a gentle reminder of the commitment they'd made to attend church every Sunday was a better idea. So instead of yelling at Juan Carlos, she said, "Baby, I can tell you're not excited about going to church today. Sometimes I feel the same way. But this is a commitment we made toward rebuilding our relationship, and it's important to me that we both keep this commitment. So please join the boys and me this week even if you'd rather stay home."

To Erica's amazement, Juan Carlos smiled and said, "Of course." Then he quickly got dressed and went to church with his family without a word of complaint. Afterward, they took the boys to the park and played for the entire afternoon. What could easily have been a huge fight and a setback in rebuilding their relationship turned out to be, because it was handled gently and empathetically, the beginning of a wonderful day together.

CHAPTER SEVEN:

Healing Your
Sexual Relationship

Following a painful sexual betrayal, many people wonder, often with fear and despair, if they will ever be able to enjoy sex with their partner.

Without question, sexuality is the most tender and personal area of our lives, and it requires tremendous vulnerability. Often, after infidelity, betrayed partners are concerned that they will never feel safe in their relationship again, and because of that they will never be able to become vulnerable enough to enjoy sex again. It's not uncommon for both parties to worry that sex will never be 'hot', or erotic while still feeling safe and comfortable.

It's important to realize that you can have a sex life that's better than ever, despite the impact of relationship betrayal, as long as you're willing to put in the work and effort. That said, a restored (and improved) sex life with your partner will not come easily or quickly. You will need to be patient and gentle as you venture into this sacred arena.

Sexuality thrives in environments where trust, vulnerability, and intimacy are present, and these are the exact parts of your relationship that were damaged by the infidelity. That is why it's so critical that you do the emotional work of healing your relationship first—before you attempt to restore your sex life. Secrets, resentments, and fears that are unresolved can paralyze a couple that is trying to reconnect sexually.

If your emotional connection is not in a good place, you and your partner will be better off talking openly, sharing about what is bothering you, and being open about your fears, needs, and desires. That is the first (and ultimately the most important) part of your commitment to recovery and healing. Brutal honesty about what is going on emotionally is the foundation for true intimacy.

If true emotional intimacy is not yet restored (or is not well on the way to being restored), you should probably hold off on trying to rekindle your sex life. Instead of actively pursuing sexual connection, put it on hold while you continue to work on emotional connection, trust, and intimacy through daily check-ins, continued recovery work, date nights, and the like—all the while knowing that eventually the time will come when you and your partner are ready for the next step.

If and when you both feel a sense of emotional intimacy and connection, and you both feel that you are ready for a renewal of your sexual connection, that's great. Follow the path laid out in this chapter to help eliminate common missteps.

Evaluate Sexual Wounding in the Relationship

The first true step toward sexual reconnection is to evaluate the sexual wounds caused by infidelity. You need to understand that sexual wounding will look different for each betrayed partner, each participating partner, and each relationship, so there is no cookie-cutter approach to identifying the damage done. Sexual wounding is unique to each person and each couple.

Consider the following examples.

- Mario and Bruni had been married for eight years when Bruni learned that Mario had been having an affair. Bruni found photos and texts of Mario's acting out partner on his phone. The other woman was the physical opposite of Bruni. Bruni was petite with a smaller chest; the other woman was curvy with large breasts. Bruni also found pornography on Mario's computer and noted a similar theme. All the images were of large-breasted women. This caused Bruni to wonder if Mario was attracted to her petite frame, and if he wanted to be with her at all.
- When Brent found out that his fiancée Andrea's infidelity involved multiple sexual partners that he knew personally, including several of his

friends, he was devastated. These men knew that he was engaged to Andrea and that he loved her deeply, and he wondered, *What must they be thinking of me? They must be laughing at me and thinking I'm a loser.* It also bothered him to think about the disrespect he thought Andrea must feel for him to be with these other men. The perceived disrespect stung his pride and he felt like the betrayal stole a piece of his masculinity.

- Stephen and Rick were married for five years when Stephen learned that Rick had been having casual sexual hookups behind his back. In a moment of honesty, Rick came clean with Stephen and told him that he'd been having sex with men he met at the gym and on hookup apps. He said that usually he received oral sex from these men. Stephen was hurt and incredibly confused. He felt that performing oral sex with Rick was a special part of their lovemaking. Now, when he imagined performing that act again, all he could think about was the other men. Stephen felt that Rick took something that was very precious to them and squandered it on strangers.

- Lacey's husband Greg went to treatment after she discovered his extensive use of prostitutes, strip clubs, and pornography. Even though she was in serious emotional pain about the betrayal, she wanted to be supportive. She had a history of addiction in her family and believed in the recovery process. After 90 days of treatment, Greg was advised by his therapist that he could now engage in the healthy sexuality outlined on his sexual health plan. Lacey, however, felt afraid. She didn't feel ready for this next step. The thought of being with Greg made her feel dirty and used. Even though she loved him, the pain around his betrayal made the idea of physical closeness repugnant. At the same time, she worried that if she didn't have sex with him, he would revert to cheating. Feelings of fear and obligation were mixed with feelings of revulsion. Lacey was confused and unsure about what to do.

- Tonya was married to Duane for 16 years when she discovered his pornography addiction. Tonya had always considered herself a sexual person, and she was very attracted to Duane. In the early years of their relationship, she and Duane had a wonderfully active sex life, though as time progressed and their children were born, this diminished. Tonya was often the pursuer of sexual intimacy in their relationship. That's why the discovery of Duane's pornography addiction was so painful for her. She was always ready and available for sexual intimacy, so why was he looking elsewhere? Was she not enough for him?

- Genevieve had an affair outside of her marriage. She and Tim, her husband of 21 years, have been working on their emotional and physical connection. However, during lovemaking, Tim cannot help but wonder if Genevieve is thinking about him or her affair partner. Just when things start to get arousing, Tim gets distracted and mental images of her betrayal get in the way of his arousal. He feels discouraged and hopeless about their sex life because of this.

These are just a few examples of how a couple's sexuality can be wounded and how damage to this very sacred area of one's relationship can linger, even after a lot of healing work has been done. Even worse, this area of relationship healing is often overlooked and not discussed. Instead, it is swept under the carpet. When that happens, the process of healing from betrayal will feel incomplete, and both partners may find that they have lingering doubts about the veracity and viability of their intimate bond.

Having open discussions around what is going on sexually with you and your partner is imperative if you hope to fully heal your relationship. That said, as stated earlier, before you dive into this work, you need to feel as if honesty and relationship trust have been restored (or that you are well into that process). You need to feel this way because sex with a person you love and care about requires a significant amount of vulnerability, and if you're not comfortable with that, you will not enjoy the sex that you and your partner are having.

Often, both the betrayed partner and the participating partner have concerns and fears that need to be addressed. The following exercise is designed to identify these issues and the thinking that underlies them. There is one table for the betrayed partner to complete, another for the participating partner to complete. You should each complete your portion of the exercise and take your responses to both your individual and couples therapists for discussion.

Sample: Evaluation of Areas of Sexual Concern

Fill out the table below. If the area of concern does not pertain to you, simply leave it blank.

Concern	Associated Cognition
Fear of Health Consequences	I can't trust that my partner is a safe sexual partner.
Body Image	My body is not attractive enough for my partner.

Betrayed Partner: Evaluation of Areas of Sexual Concern

Concern	Associated Cognition
Fear of Health Consequences	
Body Image	
Feelings of Desire	
Insecurities about Performance	
Feelings of Obligation	
Sexual Shame	
Sexual Dysfunction	

Concern	Associated Cognition
Inability to Trust	
Fear of Being Vulnerable	
Comparison to Others	
Intrusive Thoughts	

Participating Partner: Evaluation of Areas of Sexual Concern

Concern	Associated Cognition
Fear of Health Consequences	
Body Image	
Feelings of Desire	
Insecurities about Performance	
Feelings of Obligation	
Sexual Shame	

Concern	Associated Cognition
Sexual Dysfunction	
Inability to Trust	
Fear of Being Vulnerable	
Comparison to Others	
Intrusive Thoughts	

Once again, it is suggested that you share your lists with both your individual and couples therapists so you can process them individually and together. When you begin to work through these issues, you begin to better understand your individual sexual needs and desires, and you start to come together again, sexually, as a couple. As this happens, you must always be mindful of the tender areas of your and your partner's hearts.

Couple's Sexual Health Plan

Creating a sexual health plan as a couple is a great way to envision your healthy sexual life together. A couple's sexual health plan is similar to the sexual health plans that are used by addicts in recovery from sex and pornography addiction. The beauty of this type of plan is that it is individualized for each relationship. It takes into account your unique needs and desires as a couple and helps you delineate what is right for you and your relationship.

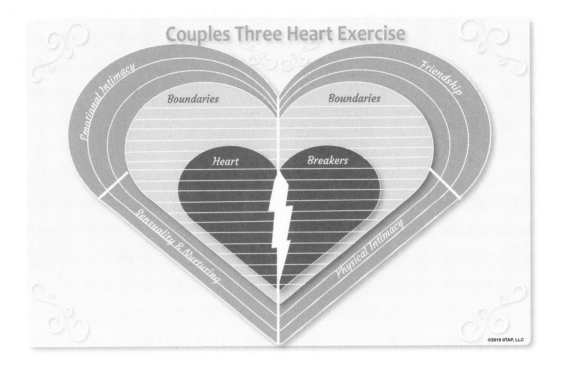

The first step as a couple is to identify areas of sexuality that may be off-limits. These are put in the center of your sexual health plan. Is there anything that, as individuals or as a couple, you do not want to participate in sexually? This list could include behaviors that you've struggled with or not enjoyed in the past. If either of you is a recovering sex or porn addict, you would also list that individual's 'bottom line' behaviors here.

These off-limits items comprise your *abstinence list*. Your abstinence list includes any sexual behavior that has been problematic or unenjoyable for either partner. Examples of behaviors that might be included in your center heart as part of your abstinence list include:

- Pornography
- Prostitution
- Affairs
- Objectifying other people
- Lying to my partner
- Using sexual hookup apps
- Using dating sites
- Going to strip clubs
- Engaging with an ex on social media
- Anonymous (or casual) sex

Your abstinence list might also include areas of pain that are still present surrounding the betrayal. For example, let's say that the betrayed partner found out that the participating partner used sex toys during the betrayal. That might be a pain point that is not yet healed. If so, sex toys might need to be included (at least for a while) on this couple's abstinence list.

It's important to keep in mind that your couple's sexual health plan is a working document. As you progress in your healing, you can mutually agree to make modifications to your plan. For example, in the case of Stephen and Rick, many of Rick's infidelities occurred by using hookup apps on his smartphone. Recognizing this, Rick using a smartphone was included in the couple's abstinence list. Rick discarded his smartphone and got a flip phone so he would not be tempted (or able) to use hookup apps. This was very reassuring to Stephen. Eventually, after about six months, when trust was almost fully restored in their relationship and Rick was stronger in his recovery, Stephen and Rick mutually agreed that Rick could go back to using a smartphone.

Create your abstinence list here:

....

....

....

....

....

....

....

The middle heart is called the *boundaries list*. This is where you decide, as a couple, on the boundaries that you need to put in place to protect your relationship. This list includes boundaries around your sexual behavior, boundaries that protect your emotional connection, and boundaries that promote safety in your relationship.

For example, when Tonya and Duane were working on rekindling their intimacy, they started to notice a negative pattern in their relationship. Whenever they discussed money before bed, it created tension between them and they would lose their feeling of emotional connection. This would cause them to turn their backs on each other, an action that created pain and disconnection for both of them. In recognition of this pattern, one of their boundaries was to not discuss money after 7 p.m.

Examples of behaviors that might be included in your middle heart as part of your boundaries list include:

- We will have filtering software on every digital device.
- No one-on-one encounters, for any reason, with members of the opposite sex (or same sex for gay relationships).
- No attending 12-step meetings when members of the opposite sex are present.
- No driving alone in a neighborhood that contains massage parlors and strip clubs.
- No staying alone overnight out of town without rigorous accountability and regular check-ins.

Create your boundaries list here:

....

....

....

....

....

....

....

....

....

....

....

....

....

....

....

The last part of the couple's sexual health plan is the outer heart, which is referred to as *healthy bonding*. This is the list of healthy behaviors that support your intimacy as a couple. This list includes four quadrants:

1. Emotional Intimacy
2. Friendship
3. Sensuality and Nurturing
4. Sexual intimacy

Emotional Intimacy

The best sex occurs when both parties feel free, open, trusting, and emotionally connected. Emotional vulnerability and physical vulnerability become intertwined and experiences become richer, more meaningful, and more fun. When you're able to give of yourself emotionally as well as physically, sex is better.

Many participating partners fall into the trap of intensity with their cheating. For example, viewing pornography that is more graphic or extreme, or having a high-risk sexual tryst. While this may feel exciting, participating partners find that emotionally it ends up disappointing and lonely. In turn, the sex also feels empty—despite the intensity. This is one of the many reasons that couples hoping to heal from relationship betrayal should work on emotional intimacy before they even think about rekindling sexual intimacy.

To this end, as a couple, brainstorm about what activities and behaviors bring you closer emotionally. For example, Brent and Andrea enjoy taking regular walks on the beach where Brent proposed to Andrea. This place is special to both of them, and it always helps them feel emotionally connected. For other couples, doing relationship check-ins every night can create emotional closeness. Sharing spirituality can also help couples feel emotionally close.

In the space below, make a list of what brings the two of you together emotionally. Then add these items to the emotional intimacy quadrant of your outer heart.

Create your emotional intimacy list here:

....

....

....

....

....

....

....

....

....

....

....

....

....

....

Friendship

This aspect of healthy bonding is all about having fun and celebrating your strengths as a couple. Similar to the list you created in Chapter Seven, what are the joyous activities that originally brought the two of you together? Examples could be things like date nights or hobbies that you both enjoy, such as taking long hikes, mountain biking, going dancing, exploring different restaurants, and going to the opera or theater. Bring your passions and your joy back into your relationship.

In the space below, make a list of what brings the two of you together as friends. Then add these items to the friendship quadrant of your outer heart.

Create your friendship list here:

....

....

....

....

....

....

....

....

....

....

Sensuality and Nurturing

A beautiful aspect of being in a relationship is experiencing the nonsexual closeness and connection that occurs. Building this aspect of healthy bonding can increase emotional intimacy and friendship in profound ways. It can also be a prelude to greater sexual intimacy. As humans, we are profoundly sensual creatures who love to be nurtured. Everyone wants to feel special, cherished, and valued. As you work on this aspect of healthy bonding, it's important that you take the time to honor how important you are to each other and how much you enjoy each other. Below are some ideas to help you with this aspect of healthy bonding. *The Couple's Guide to Intimacy: How Sexual Reintegration Therapy Can Help Your Relationship Heal* by Drs. Bill and Ginger Bercaw is another great resource for building emotional and sexual intimacy.[1]

- **Skin-Time:** One thing that can be very special for couples is to lay in bed naked, caressing one another with no sexual intent. This is simply an opportunity to enjoy cuddling and being naked and vulnerable with one another, and to enjoy each other's touch. Tickling one another's backs or arms can be enjoyable. If you feel ready to try this as a couple, try doing it several nights per week before you go to sleep.
- **Sensual Massage:** Grabbing the massage oil and taking turns giving and receiving massage is a wonderful way to build erotic tension while providing love, nonsexual touch, and intimate care. For another option, lay head to foot and massage one another's feet.

- **Sensual Bath:** If you happen to have a tub that's large enough, enjoying it together can be a wonderfully intimate experience. Use soap or bath oils to massage one another.
- **Sharing Fantasies:** A little sensual pillow talk can be a fun way to spice up your relationship. Try looking into one another's eyes and sharing fantasies about what you'd like to do to each other.

These are just a few examples. In the space below, make a list of whatever it is that brings the two of you together sensually. Then add these items to the sensuality and nurturing quadrant of your outer heart.

Create your sensuality and nurturing list here:

....

....

....

....

....

....

....

....

....

....

Sexual Intimacy

This quadrant sounds like it would be self-explanatory. After relationship betrayal, however, that is not necessarily the case. In this section, you delineate what you are ready for sexually as a couple. It's possible that one or both of you may not be ready to move into sexual intimacy at all. There might also be specific behaviors, perhaps even things that you both used to enjoy, that trigger a re-experiencing of betrayal trauma. If so, you need to be fully honest about this, remembering that your sexual health plan can always be amended later, as healing progresses.

Whatever it is that you are and are not comfortable with, this is your opportunity to talk about it and to agree on what you're ready to do. This may include everything from kissing and fondling to mutual masturbation, or oral, anal, and genital intercourse.

Keep in mind that some partners may feel like they are ready to be sexual, only to get triggered and need more time. It is important that you are willing to be patient and understanding with one another. If you need to back away from sex for a while to further build emotional intimacy, please do so. You can always re-engage with sexual activity later.

In the space below, make a list of sexual behaviors that you feel ready for as a couple. Then add these items to the sexual intimacy quadrant of your outer heart.

Create your sexual intimacy list here:

....

....

....

....

....

....

....

....

....

....

....

....

....

....

....

....

....

....

....

....

....

Now that you have created your lists, transfer your answers to the worksheet on the following pages.

Couples Three Heart Exercise

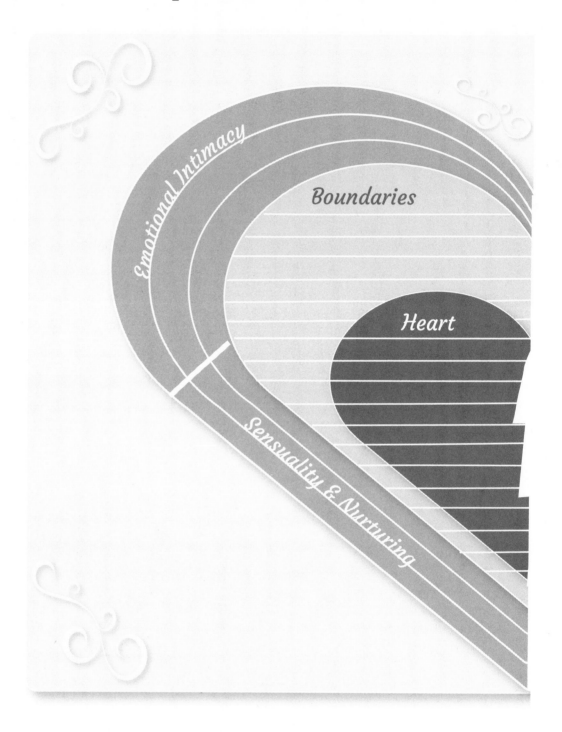

Couples Three Heart Exercise

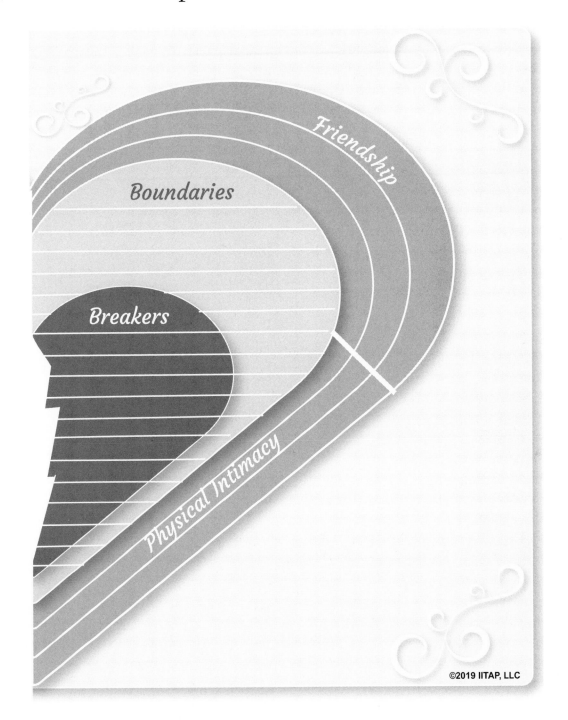

Friendship

Boundaries

Breakers

Physical Intimacy

©2019 IITAP, LLC

Getting Triggered in the Moment

It's not uncommon for one or both partners (though it occurs more often with betrayed partners) to experience fear or emotional pain in the heat of the moment when attempting sexual reintegration. This is normal. Intrusive thinking, hyper-vigilance, and fear are normal PTSD responses, and they can come up anytime there's a trigger.

If this occurs, it's important to stop, step back from sex, and focus on emotional connection. If you are triggered in this way, it's up to you to stop the action and to openly share your fear and pain. If you are the non-triggered partner, I suggest you use the SUPPORT model to respond, eventually asking your partner if you can hold him or her in a nonsexual way to provide love, patience, understanding, and reassurance.

CHAPTER EIGHT:

Moving Forward

Couples in recovery from sexual betrayal often make a devastating mistake on their healing journey. They seek treatment for the betrayal, and then, when things calm down and the crisis abates, they stop going to therapy. As mentioned numerous times in this book, all couples have underlying dysfunction in their relationships. As such, one of the most proactive steps you can take for protecting your relationship is to do ongoing work on it—even after the betrayal is resolved.

Now that you have had an opportunity to work through some of the pain of the betrayal, it is time to turn your attention to other issues in your relationship. This does not mean that the pain of the betrayal is completely in the past. From time to time it may resurface. But hopefully with the new understanding and skills you have achieved as a couple, you can begin to work on other facets of your relationship.

As you and your partner engage in this 'next-level' relationship work, it's important that you understand that no relationship is perfect and no partner is perfect. If you're insistent on perfection, your expectations are not realistic; you just won't find perfection with another human being. The best you can hope for is to feel an emotional and sexual bond with your partner, and for the things you like/love about your partner to outweigh the things that drive you crazy.

It's possible you're reading this section and thinking, *We've been asked to run ourselves through an emotional meat grinder, and now we're being asked to take it to another level by addressing all the little annoyances in our relationship?* If so, what you're feeling is totally understandable, and you may need to step away from this emotionally painful work for a short while—three months is usually a good timeframe. After that break, however, you need to get back to work, because minor irritations and resentments will linger and grow if they are not addressed. So get back in couples counseling and continue to work on communication, emotional intimacy, understanding, and connection. If you do this in good faith, your relationship can become stronger than it ever was prior to the betrayal.

Hope for Your Revitalized Relationship

As you read and do the work suggested in this book, it's likely that you and your partner will feel, at times, disheartened. That is normal and perfectly understandable. Betrayal is an emotional nightmare, and the process of healing is not easy. You'll find yourself on a relationship rollercoaster. Your partner will be on a relationship rollercoaster, too. And it won't be the same rollercoaster. Just when you're feeling great, your partner will be miserable. Just when you're feeling connected, your partner will ask for space. Just when you think you're finally ready to rekindle your sexual relationship, your partner won't be.

The good news is that this doesn't last forever. Usually, overtime, provided the participating partner has stopped the problematic behaviors and become rigorously honest, and both of you are doing the other things needed to heal yourselves and your relationship, trust within the relationship will be restored and intimacy will blossom. One morning, you'll wake up and realize that you feel good about your relationship. You're willing to be vulnerable again within the relationship, and you're happy that you suffered through the hard work of healing because now, somehow, your relationship is what you always hoped it would be.

This may not seem possible while you're in a state of upheaval caused by the betrayal, but it can and will happen if you are willing to be honest, open-minded, and diligent about the process of recovery and healing. Please, take heart, push through the tough moments, and work on your relationship.

Daniel and Monica

Daniel and Monica have been married for 17 years and have four kids ranging in age from 8 to 15. Daniel is very close to his mother and has been for his entire life.

Monica feels that Daniel's mother enmeshment is a detriment to their relationship. She says, "Sometimes I wonder if I married one person or two. It's not that I mind having a mother-in-law, but she puts herself in the middle of our marriage, and Daniel always sides with her. Whenever Daniel and I disagree about something, he turns to her. That's not what I signed up for when we got married."

At the same time, Daniel complains that Monica is as enmeshed with their four children, especially their youngest son, as Daniel is with his mother. He says, "With Monica, it's all about the kids. If I've had a really horrible day and need some comfort, it's not there. She's too busy helping the kids with their homework, their social lives, and whatever else it is they're doing. And a lot of the time, I think they really wish she'd just leave them alone for a little while. Except maybe our youngest. He'd let her do everything for him for the rest of his life. And she talks about *me* being enmeshed."

A year ago, while Daniel was at work and the children were at school, Monica met another father at childcare. Initially, their chats were friendly exchanges, laughing and swapping stories about their children. Eventually, since they only lived an hour apart, they decided to meet for coffee at a half-way point. Over coffee, they talked about the issues in their marriages. Neither of them had any intention of starting an affair, but that's what happened.

Three months later, Daniel found texts, sexts, and other evidence of Monica's ongoing affair. He reacted with a mixture of rage, sadness, and self-blame. Monica admitted what she'd done, ended the affair, entered both individual therapy and couples therapy with Daniel, and threw herself into the work of healing their marriage. Meanwhile, Daniel found an online support group for betrayed partners to help him deal with his feelings, went to couples counseling with Monica, and did his best to trust that his wife was now being honest and forthright with him in all aspects of her life. The arduous process of rebuilding trust was helped along significantly by the process of formal therapeutic disclosure.

Today, Daniel and Monica feel that they've worked through most of the trauma and mistrust created by Monica's affair. But their relationship is still rocky, with numerous disagreements and pitfalls. It seems the main issues are the same as before the affair—Daniel's enmeshment with his mother, and Monica's enmeshment with the children. Having these 'extra people' in the middle of their relationship is causing both partners to feel unappreciated, undervalued, and, at times, unloved. Both are wondering if the work of healing from betrayal has been wasted.

Attachment-Based Couples Therapy

Dr. Sue Johnson states that the most important thing in our relationships is that we feel loved, cared for, and secure.[1] When we don't feel these things, we protest and it creates conflict. This means that couples who are struggling, as we see with Daniel and Monica, need more from couples counseling than the accountability, problem-solving, and conflict management skills they learn while healing from betrayal. These couples also need to focus on and find ways to nurture the sense of attachment and comfort that they each want and desperately need from their relationship.

Changing the focus of longer-term couples work in this way—moving from crisis resolution to the development of meaningful attachment—guides us toward each partner's deepest desires and strongest emotions. Often, this work is performed using what is called Emotionally Focused Couples Therapy (EFT). This methodology, developed by Dr. Sue Johnson, has proven to be highly effective for couples dealing with both in-the-moment crises and longer-term underlying issues.[2]

EFT recognizes the value of feeling securely connected in relationships. It also recognizes that most of the drama that plays out in any relationship is only superficially about the in-laws, the children, money, or whatever else it is that a couple is dealing with in the moment. EFT understands that what really matters in a relationship is that the partners are there for each other in times of need, that each partner feels as if he or she matters to the other partner. Without this sense of secure attachment, secondary issues (such as external enmeshment, as we see with both Daniel and Monica) can take over a relationship.

If you do not feel secure attachment with your partner, you are likely to rely on one of two coping strategies.

1. You will actively blame your partner for the problems in your relationship.
2. You will numb your attachment needs and avoid engagement and conflict.

Both strategies are (misguided) attempts to create or hang onto a sense of secure attachment with your partner, and both strategies are counterproductive in that regard. The first strategy, blaming your partner, threatens and pushes your partner away, especially if this is your go-to tactic. The second strategy shuts your partner out rather than inviting your partner in. Either way, you suffer, your partner suffers, and your relationship suffers.

With Daniel and Monica, for example, both partners want to feel a secure loving attachment but neither is getting that need met. This is because, now that they've (mostly) worked through the trauma of betrayal, they're focused on their surface issues instead of what really matters. Both partners feel that they are not being prioritized by the other. Both partners feel like their needs don't matter. As a result, they continually fall into the same basic surface arguments, repeating the steps of those arguments as if they're dancing a dysfunctional, highly unpleasant waltz.

When the same old unproductive arguments repeat themselves over and over in your relationship, attachment-focused couples therapy (like EFT) is in order. It is only through hard work that you will be able to identify your problematic relationship patterns and actively work on resolving them.

Being proactive in this way is critical to the long-term success of your relationship. A relationship that has been made more fragile by betrayal cannot withstand painful arguments that go nowhere. So it's important to get back in couples therapy to resolve your underlying relationship issues. (If you are searching for an attachment-focused couples therapist, clinicians certified in Dr. Johnson's EFT process can be located at: https://members.iceeft.com/member-search.php.)

As you move forward with couples therapy to resolve your deeper relationship issues, it may be helpful for you and your partner to create a list of the issues, hurts, and unmet needs that have been covered up, ignored, or pushed aside in your relationship both before and after the betrayal. What are the hot topics and unresolved issues you have as a couple?

Our List of Core Issues for Attachment-Focused Couples Therapy

Daniel defers to his mother on every issue.
Monica coddles our children, especially the youngest, and ignores my needs.

Once you have identified the core issues in your relationship, it is helpful to identify the common processes—the ways in which these issues play out. Imagine you are evaluating your relationship at a very high level. What are the key triggers that cause arguments? Can each of you identify the feelings that underlie these triggers and cause you to get upset? What is your response?

Betrayed Partner's List of Triggers

Trigger	Feeling	Response
Our son is disrespectful and Monica gets angry at me for trying to discipline him.	*I feel shame about not being a good enough parent.*	*I get defensive and accuse Monica of coddling our kids. Sometimes I use her betrayal of our relationship as a weapon.*

Trigger	Feeling	Response

Participating Partner's List of Triggers

Trigger	Feeling	Response
I'll do something that Daniel doesn't like, and he'll call his mother to ask how she thinks I should behave.	I feel jealous that he seems to value his mother's opinion over mine. I also feel devalued and dismissed.	I get angry and use the fact that Daniel is close to his mother to belittle him.

Trigger	Feeling	Response

When you have completed these lists, bring them to your couple's therapist. Keep in mind that working on these issues is a long-term, often lifelong process. Actively working on these issues over the months and years can help your coupleship become and remain strong while also helping to prevent further infidelity. As the old saying goes: Relationships are hard work, but with this work you reap the rewards of a long-term connection.

Healing Underlying Trauma Issues

Nearly every person has experienced a significant amount of trauma in his or her life. In healthy families and situations, that trauma is quickly acknowledged, validated, and processed. In such cases, it holds relatively little sway in the traumatized person's future life. Unfortunately, when trauma is not dealt with in this healthy way, especially during our formative years, it sticks around, festers and wreaks havoc at a later point in time.

This is especially likely with participating partners, particularly in cases of compulsive sexual behavior and problematic porn use. Usually, these individuals learn early in life—courtesy of neglectful, abusive, or inconsistent parents—that their emotional needs may or may not be met by their supposedly loving caregivers. Rather quickly, they learn that when they turn to others for emotional validation and support, they're as likely to be ignored or rejected (which makes them feel even worse than they already do) as they are to receive the comfort that they crave and need.

Over time, they decide that rather than becoming vulnerable with other people, it's easier and emotionally safer to numb out with an addictive substance or behavior. Rather than trying to get their needs met through connection with other people, they push their needs to the side by getting high or creating an emotionally and psychologically intense situation that (temporarily) distracts them from the pain of their unmet needs. Eventually, this pattern of seeking intensity rather than intimacy turns into an addiction. In the case of sex and porn addiction, this will manifest as any of a thousand different forms of relationship betrayal.

Even though betrayed partners can't help but feel that their participating partner's actions are directed at their perceived or feared shortcomings, that is very rarely the case. Usually, a participating partner's actions are more about his or her unresolved early-life trauma than anything else. Sure, ongoing relationship issues may be involved, but, in a general way, compulsive and addictive sexual behavior is nearly always the result of dysfunctional lessons the participating partner learned in childhood rather than anything the betrayed partner has or has not done in the relationship.

In recognition of this fact, the participating partner may need therapy that is unrelated to relationship betrayal. He or she may need to engage in trauma therapy that addresses his or her unresolved early-life issues. This work is best done after the participating partner has stayed away from problematic sexual behaviors for several months and developed a solid recovery support network. Trauma work should be put off until that stage of healing because it is highly triggering and can easily lead to relapse.

At the same time, participating partners need to understand that betrayed partners may also have unresolved childhood trauma that's impacting them as adults. If that is the case, then a betrayed partner's in-the-moment reactions to cheating may be as related to early-life trauma as to the relationship betrayal. If a betrayed partner was neglected, abused, abandoned, or experienced some other form of dysfunction early in life, that individual's sense of safety in relationships may be diminished, leading to struggles with coping with emotions as an adult.

In such cases, the betrayed partner may, like the participating partner, need to engage in therapy that addresses his or her unresolved early-life trauma. This work can be undertaken at any time in the healing process, but usually it is put off until the relationship has healed to the point where it seems to be on solid ground. In other words, it's usually best if the immediate trauma of relationship betrayal is addressed before the lingering effects of childhood trauma are uncovered and processed.

There are many wonderful trauma treatments that can help both participating partners and betrayed partners walk through their childhood pain, including eye movement desensitization reprocessing (EMDR), somatic experiencing, sensorimotor psychotherapy, internal family systems work (IFS), post-induction therapy, psychodrama, art therapy, and more. If and when one partner decides to engage in this emotionally painful work, the other partner will need to step back from judgment and provide empathetic support, accepting that trauma resolution is an emotionally volatile process and their significant other might, at times, struggle through it.

Both Daniel and Monica realized as part of their longer-term, post-betrayal couples counseling that unresolved issues from childhood were driving a wedge into their adult-life relationship. Daniel's deepest and most painful issues primarily stemmed from having an alcoholic, verbally abusive father. Daniel says, "My dad wasn't around the house very much, and when he was home, he spent most of his time telling my mom and me how awful we were. The house wasn't clean. I wasn't good enough at sports. The dog pooped in the yard and we hadn't cleaned it up yet. Anything at all that he could pick us apart with, he did."

Is it any wonder that Daniel learned to always turn to his mother for love, support, and guidance? Is it any wonder that he feels as responsible for his mother's happiness and wellbeing as his wife's? Many of Daniel's issues could be traced back to childhood.

Monica's adult-life enmeshment with her children was also linked to unresolved childhood trauma. When she was 11, her mother left the house, moving to another city to live with a man she met through her job. At that point, as the oldest child, Monica was forced into the role of caregiver for her three younger siblings. The only parenting she received was instruction from her father on what to make for dinner, how she needed to do a better job of helping the younger children with their homework, and how he wanted his work pants and work shirts to be ironed. She says, "The only affection or validation I ever got was from my siblings, especially Joey, the baby. He made me feel like I mattered." Is it any wonder that Monica now seeks the same type of validation from her own children, especially the youngest?

Daniel and Monica, in conjunction with ongoing couples therapy, both sought individual therapy with trauma specialists to better understand and work through their unresolved early-life issues. With this work, they were able to understand themselves better, in particular the ways in which their childhoods were leaking over into their adult behaviors.

With a better understanding of why his mother's opinion and approval were so important to him, Daniel was able to revere her without continually inserting her into his relationship with Monica. And Monica, with a better understanding of her own family dynamics, was able to give her children some (much needed) emotional and psychological breathing room, and to focus that extra attention on supporting her husband.

As Daniel and Monica slowly integrated these changes into their lives and relationship, the dysfunctional arguments they used to have over and over occurred less and less often. After about two years, those arguments faded away completely.

Envisioning a New Relationship

No matter how much work you do on your relationship after betrayal, it will never be the same as it was before the betrayal. As much as you may pine for those days, it's just not possible. But that does not mean that your relationship can't become just as good or even better than it was before. In fact, many couples, after doing the work described in this book, including the extended work of addressing early-life trauma and secondary relationship issues (like Daniel and Monica did), find that their sense of intimacy, connection, and even their enjoyment of sex together is greatly increased.

Many couples choose to engage in some sort of ritual to signal the end of their old relationship and the beginning of their new relationship. This should occur only after there's been clear behavior change on the part of the participating partner, there's been honest forgiveness for relationship transgressions, and relationship trust has been rebuilt.

Typically, this type of ritual has two facets:

1. Symbolically discarding the old relationship, including the betrayal.
2. Creating a vision for the new relationship and welcoming that relationship into your lives.

These tasks can be done in any number of ways. Slightly more than two years after initial discovery of the infidelity, Monica and Daniel chose to celebrate their wedding anniversary by gathering up all of the materials related to the betrayal—anything in their lives that reminded them of the cheating—and burning those items in their backyard firepit. Then they gathered the ashes, placed them in a shoebox, buried them beneath a flower bed, and planted several rose bushes to signal a new beginning. They also exchanged private vows of fidelity, complete honesty in all aspects of life, and a willingness to continually work on the emotional and psychological intimacy in their relationship.

After that ceremony, Daniel and Monica went into the house and painted an entire wall in their kitchen with chalkboard paint. Then they labeled the wall-sized chalkboard their "Family Dream Chart" and created vertical columns for the family as a whole and each individual member of the family. They did this to create a vision board for their lives moving forward, and to help with communication about each person's need and desires.

Interestingly, the second half of this ceremony proved far more meaningful to Daniel and Monica than the first. Perhaps this is because their Family Dream Chart led them, in a way that was enjoyable not only for the two of them but for their entire family, into what marriage experts Drs. John and Julie Gottman (Gottman.com) believe are the most important aspects of lasting romantic connection: supporting one another's dreams and sharing a common vision for life.[3] The Gottmans' approach to building healthy relationships involves:

- Each person sharing honestly about his or her hopes, values, convictions, and aspirations.
- Creating a shared vision for the relationship.
- Knowing your partner's inner psychological world—his or her history, worries, stresses, joys, and hopes.
- Sharing fondness, admiration, and respect. Cherishing your partner's good qualities, while accepting his or her shortcomings as an integral part of the person you love.
- Openly sharing your need for connection and trusting that your partner will be there for you when you do this.
- Understanding individual and collective goals and working together to reach those goals.
- Recognizing that even when there is conflict in the relationship, you are on the same team. In other words, recognize that you're fighting 'the problem' rather than fighting each other.
- Committing to a lifelong journey together, knowing there will be rough patches that you will need to work through.

The Gottman's approach to couples therapy is another excellent, evidence based method for long term work on your relationship. To find a Gottman certified couple's therapist visit https://gottmanreferralnetwork.com/.

Considering the importance of moving on from the betrayal and setting up a new vision of your relationship, it is suggested that you and your partner create a ritual for moving forward that is meaningful to both of you as individuals, and to the pair of you as a couple. To help with this process, the following worksheets are provided.

5 Year Individual Vision Plan

Name: _____

Directions: Use this worksheet to identify your most important goals in the following six domains.

WORK / CAREER	PASSION / CREATIVITY	RELATIONSHIP

SELF-CARE / RECOVERY PRACTICE	SPIRITUALITY	FINANCIAL / MATERIAL GOALS

© 2019, IITAP LLC, S. Carnes

Name: _____

5 Year Individual Vision Plan

Directions: Use this worksheet to identify your most important goals in the following six domains.

WORK / CAREER	PASSION / CREATIVITY	RELATIONSHIP

SELF-CARE / RECOVERY PRACTICE	SPIRITUALITY	FINANCIAL / MATERIAL GOALS

© 2019, IITAP LLC, S. Carnes

Shared Vision Worksheet

Directions: Use this worksheet to identify your shared vision of your life together. Start by contrasting your personal vision work and then identify what aspects overlap or supplement one another. A key question to further ask yourselves is what vision do you have as a couple or family that is not reflected in either person's vision work.

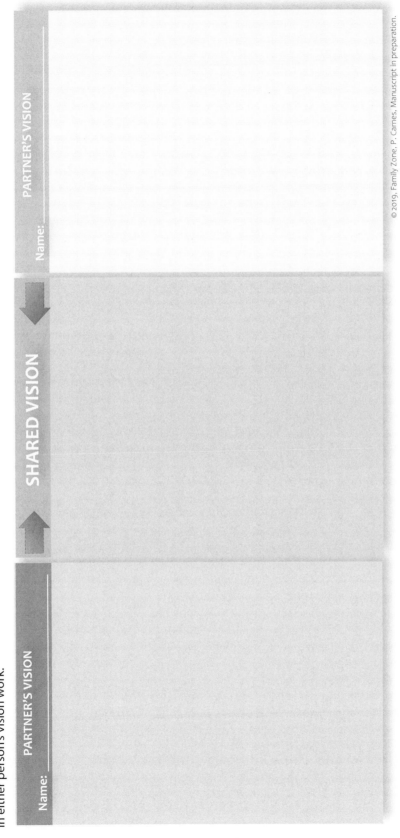

PARTNER'S VISION

Name: _____

SHARED VISION

PARTNER'S VISION

Name: _____

© 2019, Family Zone. P. Carnes, Manuscript in preparation.

In the space below, describe what this ritual will look like, and why it's important and meaningful to the two of you.

....

....

....

....

....

....

....

....

....

....

Better Than Ever

It's been said several times throughout this book that if you take the steps toward healing outlined herein, your relationship can eventually become better than ever. No, it won't be the same as it was before the betrayal, but do you even want that? Probably not. After reading this book, doing the work of healing, and recognizing that there are issues beyond betrayal that have needed to be addressed for a long time, you probably don't want your old relationship back. What you want is a new relationship built on trust, honesty, vulnerability, and intimate knowledge of one another.

This is not only possible, it's likely. If you and your partner are committed to one another and your relationship, you will do the work of healing. And with that, the anxiety and tension in your household will diminish. This does not mean that your relationship will be perfect or that you will never again fight, quibble, or become frustrated with one another. It simply means that you will no longer question if you want to stay or go, if your partner wants to stay or go, and if you are capable of overcoming the current difficulty. Because after surviving and working past the trauma of infidelity, you know that you and your partner can (and will) stay together no matter what. You also know that you have the tools to make that happen.

The best is yet to come in your relationship. The past is the past, and the future is what you make it. If you choose to make it great, you will. If you choose to stay together, to forgive, and to move forward into a wonderful new relationship filled with intimacy, trust, and love, you will achieve that goal. When the path looks darkest, be courageous and move forward toward connection with your partner. If you do so, you will be glad you did.

Resource Guide

Adult Children of Alcoholics
310-534-1815
www.adultchildren.org

Affair Recovery
888-527-2367
https://www.affairrecovery.com/

Al-Anon
888-425-2666
www.al-anon.org

Alcoholics Anonymous
212-870-3400
www.aa.org

Beyond Affairs Network
360-306-3367
https://beyondaffairsnetwork.com/

Bloom for Women
https://bloomforwomen.com/

Carol the Coach
Online Course: Post Traumatic Growth
https://carol-the-coach.teachable.
com/p/partners-find-your-post-
traumatic-growth/?preview

Co-Dependents Anonymous
602-277-7991
www.coda.org

COSA
866-899-2672
www.cosa-recovery.org

Co-Anon
480-442-3869
www.co-anon.org

Cocaine Anonymous
310-559-5833
www.ca.org

Debtors Anonymous
781-453-2743
www.debtorsanonymous.org

Emotions Anonymous
651-647-9712
www.emotionsanonymous.org

Families Anonymous
847-294-5877
www.familiesanonymous.org

Gamblers Anonymous
626-960-3500
www.gamblersanonymous.org

Gottman Referral Network
https://gottmanreferralnetwork.com/

In the Rooms: A Global Recovery Community
800-817-9497
https://www.intherooms.com/home/

International Centre for Excellence in Emotionally Focused Therapy (ICEEFT)
613-722-5122
https://iceeft.com/

International Institute for Trauma and Addiction Professionals (IITAP)
480-575-6853
www.iitap.com

Marijuana Anonymous
800-766-6779
www.marijuana-anonymous.org

Narcotics Anonymous
818-773-9999
www.na.org

Nicotine Anonymous
469-737-9304
www.nicotine-anonymous.org

Overeaters Anonymous
505-891-2664
www.oa.org

POSA
https://www.posarc.com/

Recovering Couples Anonymous
877-663-2317
https://recovering-couples.org

S-Anon
615-833-3152
www.sanon.org

Sex Addicts Anonymous
713-869-4902
www.sexaa.org

Sex and Love Addicts Anonymous
210-828-7900
www.slaafws.org

Sexaholics Anonymous
615-370-6062
www.sa.org

Sex Help (Sexual Addiction Resources)
480-575-6853
www.sexhelp.com

Sexual Compulsives Anonymous
212-606-3778
www.sca-recovery.org

Society for the Advancement of Sexual Health
610-348-4783
www.sash.net

Survivors of Incest Anonymous
877-742-9761
www.siawso.org

Recommended Reading

ADDICTION

P. Carnes, S. Carnes and J. Bailey, *Facing Addiction* (Carefree, AZ: Gentle Path Press, 2011).

C. Clark, *Addict America: The Lost Connection* (Self-Published, 2011).

G. Mate, *In the Realm of Hungry Ghosts: Close Encounters with Addiction* (Berkeley, CA: North Atlantic Books, 2008).

C. Nakken, *The Addictive Personality: Understanding the Addictive Process and Compulsive Behavior* (Center City, MN: Hazelden, 1998).

BETRAYAL

S. Arterburn and J. Martinkus, *Worthy of Her Trust: What You Need to Do to Rebuild Sexual Integrity and Win Her Back* (Colorado Springs, CO: WaterBrook Press, 2014).

P. Carnes, *The Betrayal Bond* (Deerfield Beach, FL: HCI, 1997).

S. Glass, *NOT "Just Friends": Protect Your Relationship from Infidelity and Heal the Trauma of Betrayal* (New York, NY: The Free Press, 2003).

M. Don Howard, *Intimate Betrayal: Hope and Healing for Couples Recovering from Infidelity and Sexual Addiction* (Self-Published, 2011).

D. Laaser, *Shattered Vows* (Grand Rapids, MI: Zondervan, 2008).

L. MacDonald, *How to Help your Spouse Heal from Your Affair: A Compact Manual for the Unfaithful* (Gig Harbor, WA: Healing Counsel Press, 2010).

E. Perel, *The State of Affairs: Rethinking Infidelity* (New York, NY: HarperCollins Publishers, 2017).

J. Schneider, *Back from Betrayal* (Center City, MN: Hazelden, 1988).

J. Schneider and B. Schneider, *Rebuilding Trust* (Deerfield Beach, FL: HCI, 1990).

J. Schneider and B. Schneider, *Sex, Lies and Forgiveness* (Center City, MN: Hazelden, 2001).

D. Snyder, D. Baucom and K. Coop Gordon, *Getting Past the Affair: A Program to Help You Cope, Heal, and Move On -- Together or Apart* (New York, NY: The Guilford Press, 2007).

S. Stosny, *Living and Loving after Betrayal: How to Heal from Emotional Abuse, Deceit, Infidelity, and Chronic Resentment* (Oakland, CA: New Harbinger Publications, Inc., 2013).

BOUNDARIES

H. Cloud and J. Townsend, *Boundaries in Marriage* (Grand Rapids, MI: Zondervan, 2002).

A. Katherine, *Boundaries: Where You End and I Begin* (New York, NY: Fireside Books, 1993).

A. Katherine, *Where to Draw the Line: How to Set Healthy Boundaries Every Day* (New York, NY: Fireside Books, 2000).

R. Lerner, *Living in the Comfort Zone: The Gift of Boundaries in Relationships* (Deerfield Beach, FL: HCI, 1995).

C.L. Whitfield, *Boundaries and Relationships: Knowing, Protecting, and Enjoying the Self* (Deerfield Beach, FL: HCI, 1993).

C. Wills-Brandon, *Learning to Say No* (Lincoln, NE: iUniverse, 2000).

A. Wilson Schaff, *Escape From Intimacy* (San Francisco, CA: Harper, 1989).

BRAIN

D.G. Amen, *Sex on The Brain: 12 Lessons to Enhance Your Love Life* (New York, NY: Three Rivers Press, 2007).

L. Brizendine, *The Female Brain* (New York, NY: Three Rivers Press, 2007).

L. Brizendine, *The Male Brain* (New York, NY: Three Rivers Press, 2011).

H. Fisher, *Why We Love: The Nature and Chemistry of Romantic Love* (New York, NY: Henry Holt, 2004).

A. Levine & R. Heller, *Attached: The New Science of Adult Attachment and How it Can Help You Find-and Keep-Love*, (New York, NY: Penguin, 2010).

S. Tatkin, *Wired for Love: How Understanding Your Partner's Brain & Attachment Style Can Help You Defuse Conflict & Build a Secure Relationship* (Oakland, CA: New Harbinger, 2011).

CO-DEPENDENCY

Anonymous, S (Denver, CO: CoDA Resource Publishing, 1995).

M., Ann. *Letting Go of the Need to Control* (Center City, MN: Hazelden, 1987).

M. Beattie, *Codependent No More: How to Stop Controlling Others and Start Caring for Yourself* (Center City, MN: Hazelden, 1986).

D. Corley and J. Schneider, *Disclosing Secrets* (Carefree, AZ: Gentle Path Press, 2002).

J. Friel, T. Gorski, J. Greenleafet al. *Co-Dependency* (Delray Beach, FL: Health Communications, 1988).

M. Hunter and Jem, a recovering codependent, *The First Step for People in Relationships with Sex Addicts* (Minneapolis, MN: CompCare, 1989).

P. Mellody and A. Miller, *Facing Codependence: What It Is, Where It Comes from, How It Sabotages Our Lives* (New York, NY: Harper & Row, 1989).

A.W. Smith, *Grandchildren of Alcoholics: Another Generation of Co-dependency* (Deerfield Beach, FL: HCI, 1988).

W.E. Thornton, *Codependency, Sexuality, and Depression* (Summit, NJ: Pia Press, 1990).

S. Wegscheider-Cruse, *Choicemaking: For Spirituality Seekers, Co-Dependents and Adult Children* (Deerfield Beach, FL: HCI, 1985).

COUPLES RECOVERY

B. Bercaw and G. Bercaw, *A Couple's Guide to Intimacy: How Sexual Reintegration Therapy Can Help Your Relationship Heal* (Pasadena, CA: CA Center for Healing, 2010).

P. Carnes, M. Laaser, and D. Laaser, *Open Hearts: Renewing Relationships with Recovery, Romance & Reality* (Center City, MN: Hazelden, 1999).

J. Gottman and N. Silver, *The Seven Principles for Making Marriage Work: A Practical Guide from the Country's Foremost Relationship Expert* (New York, NY: Harmony Books, 1999).

J. Gottman, *The Science of Trust: Emotional Attunement for Couples* (New York, NY: W.W. Norton & Company, Inc., 2011).

J. Gottman and N. Silver, *What Makes Love Last?: How to Build Trust and Avoid Betrayal* (New York, NY: Simon & Schuster Paperbacks, 2012).

A. Katehakis, *Erotic Intelligence: Igniting Hot, Healthy Sex While in Recovery from Sex Addiction* (Deerfield Beach, FL: HCI, 2010).

W. Kritsberg, *Healing Together: A Guide to Intimacy and Recovery for Co-Dependent Couples* (Deerfield Beach, FL: HCI, 1989).

E. Marlin, *Relationships in Recovery: Healing Strategies for Couples and Families* (San Francisco, CA: Harper, 1990).

E. Perel, *Mating in Captivity: Unlocking Erotic Intelligence* (New York, NY: Harper, 2007).

T. Real, *The New Rules of Marriage: What You Need to Make Love Work* (New York, NY: Ballantine, 2008).

D. Schnarch, *Passionate Marriage: Sex, Love, and Intimacy in Emotionally Committed Relationships* (New York, NY: W.W. Norton & Co., 1997).

S. Tatkin, *Wired for Love: How Understanding Your Partner's Brain and Attachment Style Can Help You Defuse Conflict and Build a Secure Relationship* (Oakland, CA: New Harbinger Publications, Inc., 2011)

S. Tatkin, *We Do: Saying Yes to a Relationship of Depth, True Connection, and Enduring Love* (Boulder, CO: Sounds True, 2018)

M. Weiner-Davis, *Healing from Infidelity: The Divorce Busting® Guide to Rebuilding Your Marriage After an Affair* (Woodstock, IL: Michele Weiner-Davis Training Corporation, 2017).

CYBERSEX ADDICTION

P. Carnes, D. Delmonico, and E. Griffin, *In the Shadows of the Net* (Center City, MN: Hazelden, 2001).

R. Weiss and J. Schneider, *Untangling the Web: Sex, Porn, and Fantasy Obsession in the Internet Age* (Carefree, AZ: Gentle Path Press, 2012).

FAMILY OF ORIGIN

C. Black, *It Will Never Happen to Me* (Center City, MN: Hazelden, 2002).

C. Black, *Changing Course: Healing from Loss, Abandonment and Fear* (Center City, MN: Hazelden, 2002).

C. Black, *Unspoken Legacy: Addressing the Impact of Trauma and Addiction within the Family* (Las Vegas, NV: Central Recovery Press, 2018)

M. Hunter, *Joyous Sexuality: Healing from the Effects of Family Sexual Dysfunction* (Minneapolis, MN: CompCare, 1992).

C. Whitfield, *Healing the Child Within* (Deerfield Beach, FL: HCI, 1987).

HEALTHY SEXUALITY

A. Katehakis, *Sexual Reflections: A Workbook for Designing and Celebrating Your Sexual Health Plan* (Los Angeles, CA: Center for Healthy Sex, 2018).

A. Katehakis and T. Bliss, *Mirror of Intimacy: Daily Reflections on Emotional and Erotic Intelligence* (Los Angeles, CA: Center for Healthy Sex, 2014).

E. Nagoski, *Come As You Are: The Surprising New Science That Will Transform Your Sex Life* (New York, NY: Simon and Schuster Paperbacks, 2015).

LOVE ADDICTION

Kelly McDaniel, *Ready to Heal: Breaking Free of Addictive Relationships, third edition* (Carefree, AZ: Gentle Path Press, 2012).

P. Mellody, A. Miller and J.K. Miller, *Facing Love Addiction: Giving Yourself the Power to Change the Way You Love* (New York, NY: Harper One, 1992).

S. Peabody, *Addiction to Love: Overcoming Obsession and Dependency in Relationships.* (Berkeley, CA: Celestial Arts, 2005).

B. Schaeffer, *Is It Love or Is It Addiction?* (Center City, MN: Hazelden, 2009).

MEN'S ISSUES

K. Adams, *When He's Married to Mom* (New York, NY: Simon & Schuster, 2007).

B. Erickson, *Longing for Dad: Father Loss and Its Impact* (Deerfield Beach, FL: HCI, 1998).

R. Fisher, *The Knight in Rusty Armor* (Chatsworth, CA: Wilshire Book Co., 1989).

S. Keen, *Fire in the Belly: On Being A Man* (New York, NY: Bantam, 1992).

T. Real, *I Don't Want to Talk About It: Overcoming the Secret Legacy of Male Depression* (New York, NY: Fireside, 1998).

G. Smalley, *If Only He Knew* (Grand Rapids, MI: Zondervan, 1982).

M. Lew, *Victims No Longer: The Classic Guide for Men Recovering from Sexual Child Abuse* (New York, NY: Harper Perennial, 2004).

PARTNERS OF SEX ADDICTS

C. Black, *Deceived: Facing the Trauma of Sexual Betrayal* (Las Vegas, NV: Central Recovery Press, 2009).

S. Carnes, *Mending A Shattered Heart: A Guide for Partners of Sex Addicts, second edition* (Carefree, AZ: Gentle Path Press, 2011).

W. Conquest and D. Drake, *Letters From a Sex Addict: My Life Exposed* (North Charleston, SC: Conquest & Drake, LLP, 2017).

M. Corcoran, *A House Interrupted: A Wife's Story of Recovering from Her Husband's Sex Addiction* (Carefree, AZ: Gentle Path Press, 2011).

C. Juergensen Sheets and A. Katz, *Help Her Heal: An Empathy Workbook for Sex Addicts to Help Their Partners Heal* (Long Beach, CA: Sano Press, LLC, 2019).

J. Spring and M. Spring, *After the Affair: Healing the Pain and Rebuilding Trust When a Partner Has Been Unfaithful* (New York, NY: William Morrow, 1997).

K. Skinner, *Treating Trauma from Sexual Betrayal: The Essential Tools for Healing* (Lindon, UT: KSkinner Corp., 2017).

B. Steffens and M. Means, *Your Sexually Addicted Spouse: How Partners Can Cope and Heal* (Far Hills, NJ: New Horizon Press, 2009).

E. VandeReis, *On the Journey: Poems of Betrayal and Hope* (Carefree, AZ: Gentle Path Press, 2018).

PORN ADDICTION

M. Chamberlain and G. Steurer, *Love You, Hate the Porn: Healing a Relationship Damaged by Virtual Infidelity* (Salt Lake City, UT: Shadow Mountain, 2011).

N. Church, *Wack: Addicted to Internet Porn* (Self-Published, 2014).

W. Maltz and L. Maltz, *The Porn Trap: The Essential Guide to Overcoming Problems Caused by Pornography* (New York, NY: HarperCollins Publishers, 2008).

K. Skinner, *Treating Pornography Addiction: The Essential Tools for Recovery* (Provo, UT: GrowthClimate, Inc., 2005).

G. Wilson, *Your Brain on Porn: Internet Pornography and the Emerging Science of Addiction* (United Kingdom: Commonwealth Publishing, 2014).

RECOVERY AND THE TWELVE STEPS

Anonymous, *Alcoholics Anonymous* (New York, NY: AA World Services).

Anonymous, *Al-Anon Faces Alcoholism* (New York, NY: Al-Anon Family Group Head Inc.).

Anonymous, *Al-Anon's Twelve Steps and Twelve Traditions* (New York, NY: Al-Anon Family Group Head Inc.).

Anonymous, *One Day at a Time in Al-Anon* (New York, NY: Al-Anon Family Group Head Inc., 1978).

Anonymous, *The Dilemma of the Alcoholic Marriage* (New York, NY: Al-Anon Family Group Head Inc., 1977).

Anonymous, *Courage to Change: One Day at a Time in Al-Anon* (New York, NY: Al-Anon Family Group Head Inc., 1992).

Anonymous, *Hope for Today* (New York, NY: Al-Anon Family Group Headquarters, 2007).

Anonymous, *Alateen—A Day at a Time* (New York, NY: Al-Anon Family Group Headquarters, 1983).

Anonymous, *Alateen—Hope for Children of Alcoholics* (New York, NY: Al-Anon Family Group Headquarters).

Anonymous, *Having Had a Spiritual Awakening* (New York, NY: Al-Anon Family Group Headquarters, 1998).

Anonymous, *Sex and Love Addicts Anonymous* (San Antonio, TX: The Augustine Fellowship, 1986).

Anonymous, *Recovering Couples Anonymous Blue Book* (Oakland, CA: Recovering Couples Anonymous, 1996).

P. Carnes, *A Gentle Path Through the Twelve Steps: The Classic Guide for All People in the Process of Recovery* (Center City, MN: Hazelden, 2012).

P. Carnes, *A Gentle Path Through the Twelve Principles: Living the Values Behind the Steps* (Center City, MN: Hazelden, 2012).

S. Covington, *A Woman's Way Through the Twelve Steps* (Center City, MN: Hazelden, 1994).

D. Griffin, *A Man's Way Through the Twelve Steps* (Center City, MN: Hazelden, 2009).

Bill P. and Lisa D., *The Twelve Step Prayer Book* (Center City, MN: Hazelden, 2004).

SEX ADDICTION

P. Carnes, *Don't Call It Love: Recovery from Sexual Addiction* (Center City, MN: Hazelden, 1992).

P. Carnes, *Out of the Shadows: Understanding Sexual Addiction* (Center City, MN: Hazelden, 2001).

P. Carnes, *Contrary to Love: Helping the Sexual Addict* (Center City, MN: Hazelden, 1994).

P. Carnes, *Facing the Shadow: Starting Sexual and Relationship Recovery* (Carefree, AZ: Gentle Path Press, 2001).

P. Carnes, *Sexual Anorexia: Overcoming Sexual Self-Hatred* (Center City, MN: Hazelden, 1997).

P. Carnes and K. Adams, *The Clinical Management of Sex Addiction* (New York, NY: Brunner-Routledge, 2002).

R. Weiss, *Cruise Control: Understanding Sex Addiction in Gay Men* (Carefree, AZ: Gentle Path Press, 2012).

R. Weiss and M. Ferree, *Out of the Dog House for Christian Men: A Redemptive Guide for Men Caught Cheating* (Palm Springs, CA: Three iii Publishing, 2018).

SHAME AND ANGER

J. Bradshaw, *Healing the Shame That Binds You* (Deerfield Beach, FL: HCI, 2005).

B. Brown, *The Gifts of Imperfection: Let Go of Who You Think You're Supposed to Be and Embrace Who You Are* (Center City, MN: Hazelden, 2010).

H. Lerner, *The Dance of Anger: A Woman's Guide to Changing the Patterns of Intimate Relationships* (New York, NY: Harper Collins, 1985).

R. Potter-Efron and P. Potter Efron, *Letting Go of Shame: Understanding How Shame Affects Your Life* (Center City, MN: Hazelden, 1989).

R. Potter-Efron, *Handbook of Anger Management* (New York, NY: Routledge, 2005).

B. Shoshanna, *The Anger Diet: Thirty Days to Stress-Free Living* (Kansas City, KS: Andrews McMeel Publishing, 2005).

SPIRITUALITY AND MEDITATION

Anonymous, *The Courage to Change* (New York, NY: Al-Anon Family Group, 1992).

M. Beattie, *Journey to the Heart* (Center City, MN: Hazelden, 1990).

M. Beattie, *The Language of Letting Go* (Center City, MN: Hazelden, 1990).

K. Casey, *Each Day a New Beginning* (Center City, MN: Hazelden, 1982).

P. Coelho and A.R. Clarke, the Alchemist (New York, NY: Harper, 2006).

E. Kurtz and S. Ketchum, *The Spirituality of Imperfection* (New York, NY: Bantam, 1993).

E. Larsen, *Days of Healing, Days of Joy* (Center City, MN: Hazelden, 1987).

B. Manning, *The Ragamuffin Gospel: Good News for the Bedraggled, Beat-Up, and Burnt Out,* (Sisters, OR: Multnomah, 2005).

S. Mcniff, *Trust the Process: An Artist's Guide to Letting Go* (Boston, MA: Shambhala, 1998).

M.S. Peck, *The Road Less Traveled: A New Psychology of Love, Traditional Values and Spiritual Growth* (New York, NY: Touchstone, 1998).

TRAUMA

M. Browne and M. Browne, *If the Man You Love was Abused: A Couple's Guide to Healing,* (Avon, MA: Adams Media, 2007).

C. Courtois, *It's Not You, It's What Happened to You: Complex Trauma and Treatment* (Self-published: 2014).

J. Crane, *The Trauma Heart: We Are Not Bad People Trying to Be Good, We Are Wounded People Trying to Heal: Stories of Survival, Hope and Healing* (Deerfield Beach, FL: Health Communications, Inc., 2017).

T. Dayton, *Heartwounds* (Deerfield Beach, FL: HCI, 1997).

T. Dayton, *Trauma and Addiction* (Deerfield Beach, FL: HCI, 2000).

T. Dayton, *The Soulful Journey of Recovery: A Guide to Healing from a Traumatic Past for ACAs, Codependents, or Those with Adverse Childhood Experiences* (Boca Raton, FL: Health Communications, Inc., 2019).

R. Gartner, *Beyond Betrayal: Taking Charge of Your Life After Boyhood Sexual Abuse,* (Hoboken, NJ: Wiley & Sons, 2005).

P. Levine and A. Frederick, *Waking the Tiger: Healing Trauma: The Innate Capacity to Transform Overwhelming Experiences* (Berkeley, CA: North Atlantic Books, 1997).

P. Walker, *Complex PTSD: From Surviving to Thriving* (Contra Costa, CA: Azure Coyote Publishing, 2013).

WOMEN'S ISSUES

R. Ackerman, *Perfect Daughters* (Deerfield Beach, FL: HCI, 2002).

H. Edelman, *Motherless Daughters: The Legacy of Loss* (Cambridge, MA: Da Capo Press, 2006).

L. Frankel, *Women, Anger, and Depression* (Deerfield Beach, FL: HCI, 1991).

N. Friday, *My Mother/Myself: The Daughter's Search for Identity* (New York, NY: Delta, 1997).

M. Grad, *The Princess Who Believed in Fairy Tales* (Chatsworth, CA: Wilshire Book Co., 1995).

C. Kasl, *Women, Sex, and Addiction* (New York, NY: Harper, 1990).

M. Maine, *Father Hunger* (Carlsbad, CA: Gurze Books, 2004).

D. Miller, *Women Who Hurt Themselves* (New York, NY: Basic Books, 1994).

D. Weiss and D. DeBusk, *Women Who Love Sex Addicts* (Deerfield Beach, FL: HCI, 1993).

End Notes

Chapter One

1   B. A. Steffens and R. L. Rennie, "The Traumatic Nature of Disclosure for Wives of Sexual Addicts." *Sexual Addiction & Compulsivity, Volume 13* (2006): 247-267.

2   D. Laaser, H. L. Putney, M. Bundick, D. L. Delmonico, and E. J. Griffin, "Posttraumatic Growth in Relationally Betrayed Women." *Journal of Marital and Family Therapy, Volume 43, Issue 3* (2017): 435-447.

3   J. M. Gottman and N. Silver, *The Seven Principles for Making Marriage Work: A Practical Guide from the Country's Foremost Relationship Expert* (New York, NY: Three Rivers Press, 1999).

Chapter Two

1   S. Carnes, "Executing a Well Managed Disclosure" (2020, In Process).

2   J. P. Schneider and B. Schneider, "Couples Recovery from Sexual Addiction and Co-addiction: Results of a Survey of 88 Marriages." *Sexual Addiction & Compulsivity, Volume 3* (1996): 111-126.

3   J. M. Gottman and N. Silver, *What Makes Love Last?: How to Build Trust and Avoid Betrayal* (New York, NY: Simon and Schuster, 2012).

Chapter Six

1   D. M. Ruiz, *The Four Agreements: A Practical Guide to Personal Freedom* (San Rafael, CA: Amber-Allen Publishing, Inc., 2018).

2   J. M. Gottman and N. Silver, *The Seven Principles for Making Marriage Work: A Practical Guide from the Country's Foremost Relationship Expert* (New York, NY: Three Rivers Press, 1999).

3   D. Laaser, *Shattered Vows: Hope and Healing for Women Who Have Been Sexually Betrayed* (Grand Rapids, MI: Zondervan, 2008).

Chapter Seven

1   B. Bercaw and G. Bercaw, *The Couple's Guide to Intimacy: How Sexual Reintegration Therapy Can Help Your Relationship Heal*, (Pasadena, CA: California Center for Healing, Inc., 2010).

Chapter Eight

1   S. Johnson, *Hold Me Tight: Seven Conversations for a Lifetime of Love* (New York, NY: Little, Brown and Company, 2008).

2   S. Johnson and L. Greenberg, "Emotionally Focused Couples Therapy: An Outcome Study." *Journal of Martial and Family Therapy, Volume 11, Issue 3* (1985): 313-317.

3   J. M. Gottman and N. Silver, *The Seven Principles for Making Marriage Work: A Practical Guide from the Country's Foremost Relationship Expert* (New York, NY: Three Rivers Press, 1999).

NOTES

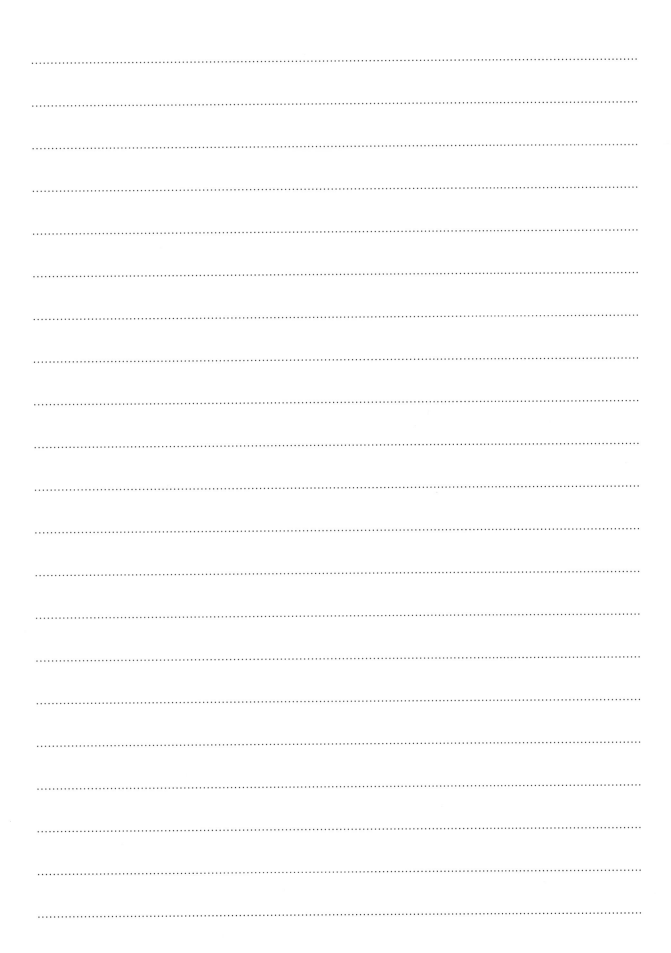